Observing Harry

Observing Harry: Child Development And Learning 0-5

Buckingham: Open University   0335213014

Observing Harry

Child development and learning 0–5

Cath Arnold

Open University Press

Open University Press
McGraw-Hill Education
McGraw-Hill House
Shoppenhangers Road
Maidenhead
Berkshire
SL6 2QL
United Kingdom

email: enquiries@openup.co.uk
world wide web: www.openup.co.uk

and Two Penn Plaza, New York, NY, 10121–2289, USA

First published 2003

Reprinted 2004

A catalogue record of this book is available from the British Library

ISBN 0 335 21301 4 (pb)   0 335 21302 2 (hb)

Library of Congress Cataloging-in-Publication Data
CIP data has been applied for

Typeset by RefineCatch Limited, Bungay, Suffolk
Printed in the UK by Bell & Bain Ltd, Glasgow

Contents

Figures and tables

Figures

Tables

Acknowledgements

First, I want to thank Ian, Colette, Georgia and Harry for allowing and encouraging me to have this story published. They have each made a huge contribution to the initial keeping of the records and to the discussion and analysis of the data. Secondly, I want to give a very special thanks to Eloise for patiently reading and re-reading the text and for giving me her honest critical feedback. I want to thank Paul and Terry for our many discussions about Harry and for being supportive in many different ways when I needed to immerse myself in writing. Lastly, I want to acknowledge the support of my colleagues at Pen Green Centre, particularly Margy Whalley, who continue to encourage me in new ventures.

Key to quotes and transcripts

Direct quotes from the parent/grandparent diary or from nursery records are italicized and in single inverted commas. Comments from parents/grandparents/workers are italicized and in double inverted commas. Transcriptions of video material are italicized, in single inverted commas and acknowledged as 'video clips' afterwards.

Introduction

This account began not as a book, but as a diary and video record of Harry's early years by his parents, Ian and Colette, and by his maternal grandparents. The author is Harry's maternal grandmother referred to in the book as Grandmop or Mop. When Harry is born his dad, Ian, works for a toy company and occasionally works away from home setting up and manning toy fairs for trades people. Like every family, we were interested in and fascinated by each new aspect of Harry's development and learning. We did not realize how much we would learn from observing and documenting what Harry did and said.

In the field of early childhood education, we draw on a long heritage of observational studies that have helped us to get to know young children and to plan for their learning (Bartholomew and Bruce 1993). Baby biographies by parents have made a major contribution to our knowledge of how children learn and how we can help them, both as parents and as educators (Darwin 1877; Navarra 1955; Piaget 1962; Matthews 1994).

One of the keys appears to be the close observation of young children by people who are deeply interested in the well-being and development of those children. Holt (1991: 133) states:

> While such close, patient observation is rare in most teachers, it comes more easily to parents, because of their interest in, and love for, their children. Like a naturalist, an observant parent will be alert both to small clues and to large patterns of behaviour.

There is also a tradition of closely observing infants and their parents in the psychoanalytic field:

> . . . we are trying to look with an observing eye at an ordinary process, at the intensity and complexity in the development of children, who are growing up to be more or less like their parents.
>
> (Miller *et al.* 1989: 4)

Within the psychoanalytic tradition, the observer reflects on the emotions evoked in them when observing an infant and his or her parents.

As Harry's maternal grandmother, I found I was fascinated by what Harry was doing at home and at the Family Centre where I work. I was excited by each new thing he did and I wanted to be involved and in tune with his deep interests. I also realized that, through observing Harry, I was able to understand theories of child development more fully. Theory, without application, seemed sterile. It was only when I applied a theory to something Harry had done that the theory became useful.

At the age of 3, Harry began attending the nursery of which I was head teacher. I began to realize just how much my intimate knowledge of Harry could benefit him and also other children in the nursery. However, having my own grandchild in the nursery was not without tensions. As part of good practice in the nursery, a key worker is allocated to each child and family (Whalley 1997, 2001). Which worker would feel confident enough to be Harry's key worker? What about when Harry was difficult at nursery? Should I intervene? Would the workers expect me to or resent my interference? Would Harry want to be with me rather than with other workers? How would I handle that situation when it arose? There was an added tension in that Harry's mother, Colette, worked in the same building. Occasionally she would walk through the nursery. Would the sudden appearance of his mother disrupt Harry's play?

We could have avoided these tensions altogether by sending Harry to a different nursery in the town without any added complications. What we chose to do was to be open to learning from others about how best to support Harry in the nursery. We found that it was important to be honest and to express our fears. When I had to deal with a tricky situation, other workers seemed to appreciate me saying how difficult I was finding it. After all, they were dealing with difficult situations every day. Flexibility was important too. Luckily, Harry's key worker, Lorna, is secure in her professionalism and can be flexible. There were no hard and fast rules. We were bound by real-life circumstances. If Harry wanted to be with me and I was free to be in the nursery, that was fine and other children benefited too. If I had a meeting, I would explain that I could not be with him and why. I would always explain and use the real reason and he seemed to understand.

There were many advantages. Harry had some speech and language difficulties and I could understand his speech more easily than people who did not know him as well as I did. I had more intimate knowledge of his home learning and could help him connect with learning at nursery (Arnold 1997). As far as curriculum planning was concerned, I could use my knowledge to ensure that we were offering appropriate open-ended resources and support to Harry and other children with similar interests. I knew the songs and stories he enjoyed at home. I knew what was happening within the family each day and I could be an advocate for Harry in all sorts of ways.

So, observing Harry became a habit and a joy. At nursery, he was observed by all of the workers when it was his turn and also when he did something a worker considered special or notable. The kinds of observations made at nursery and at home were pure, descriptive accounts of his actions and language like the observations made by Susan Isaacs in the Malting House School, Cambridge, early in the twentieth century (Isaacs 1930, 1933).

This book begins in Chapter 1 with 'Getting to know Harry and his family'. We need to understand Harry's history within his family to see where he is in his development and learning. Chapter 2 introduces the observation technique and tools and the theories of child development that will be used to analyse the observations of Harry throughout the book. The next six chapters link Harry's actions and language with the six curriculum areas that make up the Curriculum Guidance for the Foundation Stage curriculum in England (QCA 2000, 2001). In Chapter 3, we consider Harry's physical development. In Chapter 4, we make links with Harry's personal, social and emotional development. Chapter 5 is about how Harry learns to communicate, uses language and becomes literate. Chapter 6 focuses on Harry's mathematical development. Chapter 7 traces Harry's creative development. Chapter 8 looks at Harry's knowledge and understanding of the world. Finally, Chapter 9 draws together Harry's explorations in terms of his interests and needs. We conclude by looking at Harry now, aged 9, his interests and what we have learned from closely observing him.

This book is underpinned by the belief that Harry learns in an integrated way. We use the observations of Harry's spontaneous actions and language as a starting point for assessing his development and learning. Each observation can be linked with several areas of the curriculum. We separate the learning into curriculum areas only for the purpose of analysis. The focus of the book is on Harry aged 0–5. Each piece of new learning has a history and we often give relevant examples when Harry is under 2 years. We try to paint as realistic a picture of Harry's early development and learning as we can. Inevitably, what emerges is a partial picture of what happens. We can only give examples from the records and our collective interpretation but we continuously draw on the theory to understand Harry's actions.

1 Getting to know Harry and his family

In this chapter, we introduce Harry and his family. Harry is 8 months old and is sitting on the floor at our house when the following observation is made:

> *'Harry spent a good ten minutes manipulating and examining an old leather pouch. Then he spent about five minutes laughing and giggling while Colette (his mum) balanced it on her head and let it fall repeatedly. She would place it on her head. He would look towards her hand as she lowered it, as though, at first, he did not realize that she had left the pouch on her head. After a few turns, he blinked as he was waiting for the pouch to fall (as though he began to anticipate that it would fall)'.*

From reading this observation, we can deduce that Harry is very interested in the pouch. We can also deduce that he does not necessarily link his mum's movement towards her head with placing the pouch on top of her head. He continues to track her hand, which, as far as he is aware, is holding the pouch. After his mum has left the pouch on her head and let it fall several times, he seems to recognize this as a sequence of events that is being repeated over and over again. He learns that somehow the pouch is left on his mum's head (or disappears from his sight) before falling off (or reappearing) and that this is a game his mum is currently playing with him. Athey (1990) states that 'the movement aspects of objects are noted before their static configuration' (p. 135). What captures and holds Harry's attention may be the 'movement' of his mum's hand rather than the object she is moving. Athey also notes that young children become interested in 'lines' before circles. What Harry is tracking is an up/down route between two points. Piaget observed his son, Laurent, from 9 months, examining 'the route before and behind him as he was wheeled down a long hall' (Piaget 1959a, cited in Athey 1990: 135). What Harry does not at first seem to understand is that the pouch is placed on top of his mum's head and left there until *she makes it* fall off by tilting her head. As Harry develops, we will see him become very interested in the cause and effect of his own actions (Athey 1990).

Eleven days later, the following observation is made:

> *'Colette is playing a game with Harry – placing the leather pouch on her head and letting it fall. Harry obviously knows that the pouch is left on her head each time. He no longer tracks her hand but looks at her head expectantly and laughs when the pouch falls'.*

Parents as their child's first educators

As parents or carers, we often devise games with our children using objects in which they show interest. We probably take what they learn for granted, but these intimate interactions are very important for babies and young children. Gopnik *et al.* (1999) say that 'it makes sense to have babies who are brilliantly intelligent learners and grown-ups who are deeply devoted to helping them learn' (p. 9). Colette is devoted to Harry. She is teaching him and he is learning something new. She is tuned into his current interest. She is 'playing a key role' as one of Harry's 'first educators' (Whalley 2001: 4).

When we, as early childhood practitioners, genuinely view parents as their children's first educators, then we recognize the importance of the vast experience each child gains within their own family. We value listening to parents on the subject of their own children. In this first chapter, we get to know about some of Harry's early experiences.

The chapter is divided into sections about:

- Harry's home and family
- Who Harry knows
- Where Harry goes
- Harry's play at home and at the family's local Family Centre

Harry's home and family

Harry is the second child in his family. When he is born, his sister, Georgia, is 2 years 3 months. His parents, Ian and Colette, have lived in a three-bedroom house in a small, circular close for several years. They know all of the other families in the close.

As their second born child, Harry is under less pressure to conform than his sister was. Like most parents, his parents feel less nervous and more confident about raising their second child than their first. Holmes (1993) notes that 'parents are more relaxed and less punitive with second children than with first-borns' (p. 51). Harry's parents have also become regular users of their local Family Centre and know lots of other parents with young children. They realize that bringing up children is not easy for anyone. Colette says about Harry:

> *"He had an easier time than Georgia. We allowed him to eat when he wanted to, come into bed with us when he wanted to. Things could have been really fraught if we had made him wear a coat. He could not bear to be restricted and would scream and resist whenever we tried to put a coat on him".*

Harry is able to make some choices from an early age. His parents listen to him and it is not a major disaster when, for example, he chooses not to wear a coat. He appears to be indicating that he likes to wear comfortable clothes. Eventually they compromise by buying him warm hats and fleece tops and tracksuits.

How Harry's home and family affect his development and learning

It is difficult to know whether Harry's determination is part of his unique personality or is something he develops through his early experiences of how other people treat him. He is valued as an individual within his immediate family. He is very different to his sister and comparisons are rarely made. His parents seem to welcome the differences. Harry seems to learn, early on, that the greatest satisfaction comes from pleasing oneself. The family are interested in getting to know him as well as helping him to get to know them. Chess and Thomas (1984: 21) introduce the idea of 'goodness of fit' to describe the relationship between a child and his environment. So if, for example, Harry had been his parents' firstborn child, they might have felt under more pressure to make him conform. They might have tried to force Harry to wear his coat. The environment his parents provide is relaxed. Harry's determination 'fits' well with his parents' relaxed attitude.

Who Harry knows

Harry's parents and sister are at the centre of his social world. He also has two sets of grandparents, who live locally, as well as aunts and uncles. The people who live in the close and the people (children and adults) that he meets at the Family Centre all become part of his social network.

How Harry's family handle his allergy to dairy products

Harry's first and most important relationships are with his mum, dad and sister, Georgia. He is breastfed and this becomes a very important part of his upbringing when Harry has an allergic reaction at 6 months old. His eyes and face swell and, at first, the family's general practitioner thinks it may be an allergy to a different soap powder, as the family are staying in a hotel while attending a friend's wedding. There is a period of worry and uncertainty until, finally, Harry is diagnosed as being allergic to dairy products. The family are given medication, which can be administered in an emergency. Ian and Colette are keen not to restrict Harry's explorations. Rather than being extra-protective towards him, they try to make sure that everyone Harry knows and is likely to be with has information about his allergy and know what to do in an emergency. Harry uses the crèche at the Family Centre, so this includes crèche workers as well as the extended family and friends.

Harry continues being breastfed until he is 1 year 7 months. At the time it seems endless but, looking back, Colette feels that it was the best start for Harry.

> *"It would have helped had we known how long it was going to last. Other people's attitudes towards breastfeeding a toddler made it difficult. People would ask 'Are you going to be breastfeeding him when he starts school?' "*

Comments like this obviously hurt their feelings. Recent evidence indicates that even very young babies know how their parents are feeling (Trevarthen 2002). So it would seem that Harry, himself, might be affected by these comments.

Harry's relationship with his sister, Georgia

Harry's relationship with Georgia is very close. Dunn (1993) reports that very young children can be in touch with what their siblings think and feel and often display their knowledge through their use of humour. The following is an illustration of Harry's understanding, at 10 months, about Georgia:

> *'. . . zoomed over to Georgia's table in his baby walker. (She had gone to bed.) He picked up her new small case of pens and paints. He held it with both hands and laughed out loud. He zoomed around the room and to the kitchen holding the case and looking very pleased'.*

Already, at 10 months, is Harry's knowledge sophisticated enough to understand that

- Georgia is in bed (or is he being an opportunist?)
- Georgia values her new pens and paints?
- Georgia does not allow him to play with them?
- He can be mischievous and humorous by showing the adults that he has Georgia's new pens?

Harry has a special blanket that he likes to hold while he is breast-feeding. Georgia has a dummy and a special doll, called Nancy, which she holds when she is going to sleep. At 1 year 1 month, Harry notices that Georgia's dummy has fallen out of her mouth as she sleeps.

> *'He picked up the dummy, had a suck, then picked up Nancy and threw her onto Georgia and placed the dummy on her chin'.*

Harry does not have a dummy. On this occasion he seems to be trying out the dummy.

A few days later, Harry notices that Georgia has put dummy and Nancy down while she is drawing:

> *'Harry went across to the table and put the dummy into his mouth, looked around, then picked up Nancy and put her on his neck (like Georgia does) and walked across the room in his babywalker'.*

This is audacious behaviour, as Georgia is awake and likely to be very cross with him for using her comforters. He is clearly taking a risk, teasing and being quite humorous. He knows that Georgia has a strong emotional attachment to these 'transitional objects' (Winnicott 1975).

When Harry is 1 year 6 months, Ian, his dad, frequently tells him not to play with the stereo. (It is expensive equipment.) Harry reacts by *'running over to the stereo, twiddles and turns all of the knobs and buttons as quickly as possible before running away from it'*. Is he being an opportunist or thinking that if he does it very quickly, no-one will notice? Is he deliberately flouting his dad's authority or being humorous? Does he think it is a risk worth taking because the buttons and knobs look so inviting? Colette thinks he was looking for a reaction and that it was about *"breaking a boundary"*.

Selective attachments

Harry is discriminating in his choice of whom he likes to spend time with. From an early age he is drawn towards the male members of the family. Naturally he misses his dad when he works away from home. At 7 months, *'Harry is really pleased to see Ian after he has been away in London for 3 days'*.

At 1 year 2 months, on holiday with his parents and grandparents, he clearly shows a preference for being with his Grandpop (grandfather):

> *'When his Grandpop came home from golf, Harry was very pleased. He touched his Grandpop's leg and foot (Grandpop had his shoes and socks off). Then Harry brought his own sandals over and touched Grandpop's foot with one of his own sandals. Colette asked what he wanted – he indicated "put sandal on Grandpop". Colette tried and showed him it did not fit. She showed him Grandpop's shoe, which was a lot bigger. Then Harry indicated that he wanted Grandpop's can of lager. Grandpop poured the contents into a glass and gave Harry the empty can. A couple of*

times Harry placed the empty can into a glass which was part full of lager – he looked around at everyone when he did this and looked pleased'.

Is Harry trying to identify with his Grandpop? When he offers his sandals, is he thinking "You've got no shoes on, you can borrow mine". Or is he using his shoes as a symbol to communicate "You need your shoes on"? Is Harry imitating his Grandpop when he 'asks' for the can of lager? Does he want to imitate the pouring? Does he enjoy putting one object inside another?

When Harry is 1 year 5 months and I am babysitting, he shows a clear preference for his Grandpop:

> *'Harry was really upset and I could not get him settled until Terry (Grandpop) came over. He changed completely when Terry arrived and began playing. He had a cuddle with Terry, then leaned over the chairs and pointed at a case of sticklebricks . . . Pulled Terry's shirt as though asking him to play'.*

At 1 year 6 months, Harry has been playing at our house, when Grandpop and Uncle Paul arrive home and he shows that he wants to be with them.

> *'Harry and Colette were about to go home when Grandpop came in the back door and, soon after, Uncle Paul came in the front door. The transformation was amazing! As soon as Harry heard Grandpop, he grabbed his new coat and immediately took it and showed it to him. It was like an icebreaker. He was very busy with money, candles and corks around Grandpop and Uncle Paul. Both sat on the couch and Harry sat between them for a while. At one point, he put his head on Paul's knee and just stayed quietly there for a while. After playing for a few more minutes, he got on Grandpop's knee and snuggled into his chest, again staying there for a while with his eyes shut'.*

The fact that Harry chose to show his Grandpop his new coat may be interpreted in several ways:

- He may just grab the nearest object to make a connection with his Grandpop?

- He may think that Grandpop will be impressed with his new coat?
- He may think that Grandpop will focus on him if he shows something related to himself?
- The way Harry behaves demonstrates that he is clearly seeking emotional support from Grandpop and Uncle Paul.

Harry also makes a close link at an early age with James, who is 2 years older than Harry and the family's next-door neighbour in the close. James is the only other boy living in the close, although there are nine girls, including Georgia. Harry and James have continued to be close friends to this day. (Harry is 9 and James is 11.)

How people affect Harry's development and learning

Harry has close emotional ties to both of his parents. At 8 months, he begins to say something, which sounds like 'Mum'. At 9 months *'Harry waved to Ian as he left for work this morning for the first time'*.

The parent diary and early video of Harry indicate that he becomes securely 'attached' to his parents and later on to other significant people (Bowlby 1969; Schaffer and Dunn 1979; Tizard 1986; Quinton and Rutter 1988; Dunn 1993; Goldberg 2000). Main (1999) describes 'the attachment figure' as 'the infant's "solution" to potentially life-threatening circumstances of an immediate kind' (p. 846). Bowlby introduces the idea of the 'internal working model' (Holmes 1993: 78). Bowlby's idea is that 'The developing child builds up a set of models of the self and others, based on repeated patterns of interactive experience'. Harry has an expectation that people will, for example, play with him. When he is 8 months old, the following observation is made,

> *'Samantha (aged 4 years) and Georgia (nearly 3 years) were near the patio doors. Harry zoomed over in his baby walker, held on to the curtain and grinned up at them expectantly. (Colette thinks that he wants to play peep-bo – a game which he has previously played with Georgia)'.*

Establishing his identity as a male

As we have seen, Harry definitely seeks out male members of the family. This may be because he is trying to establish his own identity as a male. Miell (in Barnes 1995: 213) notes:

> Whiting and Edwards (1988) have examined the ways in which young children in different parts of the world become fully integrated into their culture and develop an understanding of the rules for behaviour considered appropriate for that culture. A very important part of this process is gender socialization, through which children become aware of the behaviour considered appropriate for girls and boys.

Miell (1995) also points out that 'Freud's work has stressed the importance of the child identifying with the same-sex parent in the development of a clear sense of gender identity' (p. 213).

Harry appears to seek out those role models who will help him to know what is expected of him within his family and culture.

Where Harry goes

Harry's parents take him and his sister to the local Family Centre to drop-in and baby massage. Harry, Georgia and their parents have been using the Centre since Georgia was a baby. Right from the start, Harry doesn't appear quite as sociable as Georgia. Whereas she will do anything to be with friends, Harry seems more discriminating about people. He, however, appears to pay a lot more attention to objects in his environment. He seems to notice new furniture, pictures or jewellery and signals his interest by staring for several seconds at anything new or different. (This interest in objects continues. When he is 7 years old, Harry often comments on buildings, especially churches, while travelling by car.)

Harry makes connections

Harry also seems to make connections between things that look similar. At 1 year 3 months:

> *'Harry pointed at the spotlight then at the main light. He pointed to outside (back garden). I opened the back door and pointed at the half moon. Harry pointed and went a little way down the garden'.*

Did Harry know the moon was out? Is he comparing the moon to the two lights?

At 1 year 6 months:

> *'Harry got out a packet of night light candles and blew towards one. He also blew towards the reading lamp. He pointed to outside and went out with me but no moon was visible. He did the same with Paul and went to the back and front of the house but the moon was not visible at all'.*

Is Harry making connections between three sources of light – candles, electric light and the moon? It may not be a coincidence that later, at 3 years 7 months, Harry is interested in **how** it becomes dark (see Chapters 7 and 8). Also much later when Harry is in infant school and the theme is 'Light and Dark', he becomes very involved in collecting resources at home to take into school. Around the same time, he also does several paintings at home and at his grandparents' house that connect with this theme (see Chapter 8).

Attending drop-in at the Family Centre

Harry attends drop-in at the local Family Centre with his mum or dad. The drop-in is well resourced and Harry often chooses to play with the maple blocks, train set or farm animals. Even here he identifies with a male member of staff. At 1 year 10 months, Harry is outside the Family Room when *'Harry leaned forward and kissed Marcus' photo'*. Marcus is one of the two male workers at the Family Centre. When Harry starts nursery, Marcus becomes a significant adult in Harry's life.

How where Harry goes affects his development and learning

> People learn, represent and utilize knowledge in many different ways . . .
>
> (Gardner 1991: 12)

We have seen that Harry is observant and readily makes connections between things that he views as similar. His parents take him out each day, to visit friends or relatives, to local parks or to the Family Centre. These trips out provide many different objects and people for Harry to observe and interact with. Harry also goes to massage, where he has the first-hand experience of being massaged, usually by his mum. Even as a baby, he expresses his wish to have only his feet massaged. At 9 years old, Harry still enjoys being massaged. He will ask his parents to massage his back first but usually ends up having his feet massaged. This seems to be what he enjoys most and he has the experience to choose what he prefers.

Building on first-hand experiences

In the previous section, we hear that Harry, at 1 year 3 months and 1 year 6 months, seems to be comparing lights, candles and the moon. This shows that Harry has first-hand experiences of seeing lighted candles and of being out after dark and seeing the moon. This illustrates how crucially important 'first-hand experiences' are to human beings. It is impossible to think and reflect without those experiences to reflect upon (Bruce 1991).

Occasionally, Harry comments on what he is noticing in his environment. At 1 year 11 months, in April:

> 'Harry went out into the garden, pointed at a Christmas Tree and said "tree". I showed him the other two Christmas trees, which had been planted. He kept going near each one, pointing and saying "tree" and "more tree". He looked at a photo in the hall and said "baby" and, pointing at himself, said "me". I told him it was Georgia. He said "Dorda". I showed him Harry as a baby on the kitchen windowsill. He carried the picture round for a while, saying "baby" and "me" (and pointing at himself). Finally, he placed it in front of Georgia's photo in the hall concealing hers behind his'.

Here Harry seems to be trying to group or classify objects and people in his environment. We had thought that these were identical photos of Harry and Georgia with us. We suddenly became aware that baby Georgia was in my arms with Grandpop alongside and baby Harry was in his Grandpop's arms with me alongside. We then began to question whether we had treated the children differently right from the start in relation to gender? Had Grandpop chosen to be close to Harry or had Harry chosen to be close to Grandpop?

Using the family room in the Family Centre

Harry's parents often take him and his sister to the family room in the Family Centre. This is a room where parents and children can drop into anytime. Children who use this room regularly develop some complex pretend games. When Harry is 2 years 3 months, he is observed in the family room:

> *'At lunchtime, the children began playing tigers, diving on each other in the cubby hole. It must be a regular game – as soon as Harry heard a roar, he got up, dashed towards the cubby hole, roared like a tiger and grabbed (?) Laura before diving into the cubby hole. (It seemed to be some sort of pretend game.)'*

Harry's play partners

Harry's parents take him to places where he has many opportunities to play with older and younger children than himself. The children that Harry plays alongside in crèche and the family room also visit Harry and his family at home. This means that he can get to know them really well and develop more complex games with them. Bruce (1997) states that there are many benefits to playing with older and younger play partners and in groups, pointing out that 'Group play involves children in giving up their immediate wishes in order that the play can continue successfully' (p. 147).

Harry's play at home and at the Family Centre

Harry uses a treasure basket

When Harry is a few months old, we put together a basket of household items for him to play with when he begins to sit up. The idea is Eleanor Goldschmied's and she calls it a 'treasure basket' (Goldschmied 1987). The basket contains a variety of items made in natural materials (not plastic). The items are mostly made of wood, metal or

Figure 1.1 Harry and his treasure basket.

glass. The idea is for babies sitting up but not yet walking to have a variety of objects to explore and investigate. As soon as Harry sits up, he begins to play with the objects in his treasure basket. His parents remember that he particularly liked manipulating a heavy metal chain.

When Harry goes to drop-in, massage or the family room, similar treasure baskets are on offer and, again, Harry enjoys manipulating and examining these objects. There are usually slight variations in what each basket contains, so, although Harry recognizes the basket, there may be new objects to explore in each one.

Harry repeats patterns in his play

When Harry becomes mobile, the parent diary shows that, at home, he often chooses to play with household items as well as with toys. He repeats patterns in his play (Athey 1990; Bruce 1997; Arnold 1999) and these patterns help us to understand what Harry is learning. The most frequently observed patterns in Harry's early play (8 months to 1 year 11 months) are:

1   Putting objects inside containers (37 observations).
2   Taking objects out of containers (18 observations).
3   Throwing objects (7 observations).
4   Carrying objects and placing them with people or in different locations (17 observations).
5   Making lines with objects (12 observations).

These patterns of play are called 'schemas'. Bruce and Meggitt (1999) state: 'Schemas are patterns of linked behaviours which the child can generalise and use in a whole variety of situations. It is best to think of schemas as a cluster of pieces which fit together' (p. 170). When Harry tries out these repeated actions on objects in his environment, then he is discovering the properties of each object, so that he builds up a mental picture of which features are necessary for the object to function or be used in a particular way.

Harry explores containment

Many of Harry's early investigations involve 'putting objects inside containers'. At first, Harry does not know which way up the container must be to function as a container. At age 10 months: '*Harry put a couple of pegs on top of the upside down container, then deliberately turned it the right way up and put some pegs inside. He did this several times*'. What makes his parents think he is doing this 'deliberately'? Is this a new piece of learning? Is he testing the outcome of his actions by repeating them 'several times'?

At 1 year 11 months, Harry has such a secure understanding of containing that he can use it to play a joke:

> '*Harry is sitting on Colette's knee drinking juice. When he has finished he pretends to tip it on Colette. He plays for a few minutes pretending to tip it on Colette, then she pretending to tip it on him. He is squealing with laughter. Suddenly, without warning, he pretends to throw it towards me and laughs. Then he puts the cup upside down on Colette's head and leaves it there.*'

To joke in this way, Harry has a sophisticated understanding of what the consequences of his actions would be if the container still contained juice. Note that Harry repeats his actions several times. Harry ends this play episode by placing the cup upside down on his mum's head. He begins and ends the game. At the beginning of this chapter, we hear that when Harry is 8 months, his mum initiates a game with him. Harry, at 1 year 11 months, seems to have taken on that initiation. (We will look at further examples from these patterns or schemas throughout the book.)

How Harry's play affects his development and learning

From an early age, Harry has the ability to concentrate and to become 'deeply involved' (Laevers 1997). His parents are interested in watching what happens when he follows his own interests. Wherever Harry is playing, whether at home, at his grandparents, the Family Centre, the park or on the train, he appears able to concentrate on exploring these early patterns (Athey 1990). He uses whatever is available to him and this includes people. The role that other people play is very important. Gopnik *et al.* (1999) note that 'Naming turns out to be connected to understanding a rather different aspect of the world' (p. 126). So when adults and other children articulate what Harry is doing while he is doing it, they are actually helping him to understand his own actions. Gopnik *et al.* add that 'early words often appear at the same time children are solving relevant new problems'. We saw in the last section that Harry frequently explores 'putting objects inside containers'. The records show that at 1 year 2 months, he says *"In there!"* with meaning. Another example is at 1 year 10 months, when Harry has been very involved in making lines of vehicles and extending them, and he points at several vehicles in turn, saying *"More, more, more, more!"* Is Harry beginning to count? Is he describing how he extends the line? Is he using a line of words? Is he beginning to understand the concept of adding on to make more?

Summary

In this chapter, we have introduced

- Harry, a determined little boy, who is intrinsically motivated to actively explore his environment from an early age.

- The people who are important to Harry.
- The play in which Harry becomes involved.

Table 1.1   Schemas mentioned in Chapter 1

On top
Up/down trajectory
Containment
Inside/outside
Arc-like trajectory
Transporting
Lines
Filling
Emptying

In the next chapter, we begin to look at Harry's explorations from different theoretical perspectives. We will examine how Harry's play can be analysed in different ways to assess his development and learning.

2 Observing Harry and using theory to understand Harry's development and learning

We observe Harry to understand what he is learning. Like Susan Isaacs in the 1920s, we make narrative observations. These tell the story of Harry's actions and language without any judgements being made about his intentions at first. This sort of observation is descriptive, looks at the whole child and does not have pre-determined outcomes. Piaget (1962) made many narrative observations of his own three children and of children in the 'Maison des Petits'. Here is an example:

> At 5;2 V. amused himself by jumping up and down on the stairs. At first he carried out his movements aimlessly, but later he tried to jump from the ground on to a seat, increasing the distance he jumped each time. K. (5;6) then did the same, but from the other side. They were eventually jumping at opposite ends, running along the bench to meet each other, one being pushed backwards by the collision.
>
> (Piaget 1962: 117)

Note that Piaget states the age of each child and that he judges V's actions to be 'aimless' at first but then observes that V and K set themselves targets. We can see immediately that these two children are amused and motivated to act. We can easily make links with their physical, mathematical and personal and social development. The observation is in sufficient detail for us to know what is happening at the time the children are observed. To make sense of our observations, we need to look at theories about how children learn and how adults can help them.

This chapter is divided into three sections:

- Looking at Harry's learning through the theories of Piaget, Vygotsky and Bowlby
- Looking at Harry's learning through contemporary theories
- Analysing narrative observations of Harry

In trying to understand Harry and other young children and their families at the beginning of the twenty-first century, we look back at the theories put forward by three very influential theorists – Piaget, Vygotsky and Bowlby.

Looking at Harry's play through different theoretical perspectives

Jean Piaget

Piaget is born in Switzerland in 1896. He is an only child. His early interest in observing molluscs in their natural habitats appears to lead him towards adopting a similar method when studying children (Piaget 1959a). Piaget becomes intrigued by children's incorrect responses to intelligence tests. Subsequently, he observes and records the spontaneous actions of his own three children. Piaget is open to discovering links between the behaviours he observes. In much the same way we can be open to discovering links between Harry's actions over time. Piaget formulates his best-known theories from his early naturalistic observations of his own children.

Piaget's major ideas

1   Knowledge is constructed by the learner.
2   Learners pass through stages of development.
3   Children display schemas (or patterns of behaviour) that are generalizable.
4   Development from one stage to the next occurs through processes that Piaget calls assimilation, accommodation and equilibration.

1 Knowledge is constructed by the learner
Piaget would say that Harry constructs knowledge from his own first-hand experiences. For example, we see in Chapter 1 that Harry spends

a lot of time 'putting objects inside containers'. On one occasion, when Harry is 1 year 1 month, he begins playing with a cup containing some spoons:

> *'He tipped them out and then began trying to put them back in, not quite managing at first. He put a spoon across the top of the cup and then could not get any of the others in. He kept trying and eventually managed. He seemed to get the hang of putting either the head or the handle of the spoon into the cup and letting go'.*

Harry is learning a kind of rule about how he needs to orientate long, inflexible objects to be able to put them into round, inflexible containers. His parents might offer him an instruction or show him how to do this, but Piaget's argument is that Harry needs to discover how to achieve this for himself. When this becomes a deliberate act, Harry practises as often as he needs to, to know that the method will always work.

Research by neuroscientists Recent research by neuroscientists supports this view. Blakemore (1998) goes as far as saying that we 'build our own brains'. He would suggest that Harry's knowledge comes from his experience of the world. Therefore, Harry's experience of putting the spoon into the cup several times on this occasion leaves an impression on his brain, which forms his knowledge of how to put spoons into cups.

Most contemporary educationalists would agree that first-hand experiences are important to Harry (Athey 1990; Lally 1991; Bruce 1997; Gopnik *et al.* 1999; Pound 1999).

2 Learners pass through stages of development
Piaget suggests that Harry's development leads his learning. He would say that Harry passes through four stages of development.

- Sensorimotor (from birth to approximately 2 years). At this stage, Harry learns through his senses and movement.
- Pre-operational (from 2 to 7 years). At this stage, Harry begins to represent his earlier actions with symbols.
- Concrete operational (from 7 to 11 years). At this stage, Harry learns to grasp abstract notions but still refers to concrete objects and activities.

- Formal operational (11 years and above). At this stage, Harry can think systematically, devise hypotheses and test them.

Piaget would argue that Harry leads his own learning and that 'adults can do little to push' Harry from one stage to another (Das Gupta in Oates 1994: 47). Although there may be some support for the theory that child development leads learning, the idea of a hierarchy of such distinct stages has been generally rejected. In her critique of Piaget's theories, Boden (1979) states: 'First he tends to overestimate the unity and distinctness of the stages. Second, Piaget tends to underestimate the complexity of children's cognitive achievements' (p. 32).

After making his original hypotheses based on his naturalistic observations, Piaget spends many years setting up clinical experiments to gain more insights. Donaldson (1987: 76) repeats many of Piaget's experiments and discovers that children function at a higher level when, what is being asked, makes 'human sense' to them. In other words, Harry demonstrates what he knows and can do in real-life situations, rather than when experiments are set up.

3 Children display schemas that are generalizable

Piaget suggests that there are universal patterns in children's play. Piaget would say that Harry tries out these patterns (or schemas) on every object he comes across in his environment. Harry is using these patterns to discover how the world operates. There has been renewed interest and a substantial amount of research into how young children learn through schemas during the last 30 years (Athey 1990; Nutbrown 1994; Meade with Cubey 1995; Arnold 1997, 1999; Bruce 1997). The Froebel Project, directed by Chris Athey, led the way in the 1970s. The Froebel Team collaborated with parents to collect evidence of schemas being explored by twenty project children over 2 years (Athey 1990). As nursery practitioners and parents, observing and being able to recognize the patterns in Harry's play (schemas) means that we can predict what he might be interested in exploring next.

How we can extend Harry's play through spotting his schemas We can extend Harry's play by offering language to accompany his actions and stories that link with his actions. For example, when Harry (aged 1 year 11 months) is making lines with jigsaws, vehicles and animals, we can make sure that

- He has space indoors and outside to extend his line as far as he wants to.
- We offer him resources and allow him to use them in his own way, for example, blocks, train track, video cases, playing cards, play people, bottles, chairs, planks, crates, boxes, scarves (a variety of materials, weights and lengths).
- We listen to what he is saying and try to 'tune in' (Stern 1985) to his interest. For example, when Harry says 'more, more, more, more, more', we can comment 'Yes, you're adding more and making your line longer'.
- We offer stories that link, for example, 'The Gingerbread Man' or 'The Elephant and the Bad Baby', in which lines of people follow each other.
- We might try to extend Harry's learning by playing 'Follow My Leader'.

Spotting these patterns in Harry's play does help us to predict what he might do next, but we must keep watching him as the patterns are complex and begin to cluster. We cannot, for example, decide on our theme for a term on the basis of observing Harry 'making lines'. Harry might quickly focus on another aspect, for example, making a line into a circle (*enclosure*) or *connecting* to extend his line. Also, as we shall see throughout the book, Harry revisits each of his action schemas when he incorporates them into his symbolic or functional play.

4 Development through assimilation, accommodation and equilibration
Piaget would say that Harry extends his knowledge by *assimilating* new content into his current schemas or models. For example, Harry gains a great deal of experience of putting objects into containers. When he '*scrunches a tissue to fit into an oxo tin*' and '*puts the head or handle of a spoon into a cup*' to fit it inside, he appears to be assimilating new content into his existing model about how objects go inside containers.

Harry accommodates new knowledge into his current model Piaget would say that when Harry (aged 1 year 7 months) puts his toys into a box and they fall out of the other end, then he *accommodates* his model to include what happens when an object, which looks like a container, has an opening at either end. Harry has this experience a few days after going to London by train and being interested in *going through* several tunnels. Subsequently, he begins to notice 'tunnel-like' shapes in the environment and to gain more experience of *going through* boundaries and putting objects through containers with openings at either end. Harry subsequently assimilates new content into his new schema or model (*going through*).

Harry's knowledge becomes stable   Equilibration occurs when Harry's new knowledge stabilizes through the feedback he receives from the environment (Boden 1979; Cohen 1983). So now Harry knows the difference between a container and a tunnel. Piaget (1980) describes 'mental development' as 'a continuous construction comparable to the erection of a vast building that becomes more solid with each addition' (p. 4). Harry is gaining a stable body of knowledge, which is constantly changing and developing and becoming more complex.

Lev Vygotsky

Vygotsky is born in Russia in 1896. He is the second of eight children. Vygotsky's main concern is with how children learn through their social interactions with other people. Vygotsky dies aged 38 and, therefore, does not have many years in which to experiment and to extend his theories.

Vygotsky's major ideas

1   Children develop by interacting with other people.
2   There is a zone of proximal (or potential) development within which children can function at a higher level with help.
3   Children develop spontaneous or everyday concepts before learning scientific concepts.

1 Children develop by interacting with other people

Vygotsky's (1986) theory about how Harry develops thought is that development consists of 'first social, then egocentric, then inner speech' (pp. 35–6). Harry is introduced to ideas and concepts firstly in a social context. He is part of his family and community and he learns from his interactions with other people. Harry internalizes these many interactions and goes through a stage of using egocentric speech. He seems to be thinking aloud when he talks to himself about what he is doing. Vygotsky (1986: 32) would view Harry's use of egocentric speech as 'an intermediate stage leading to inner speech' or thought. So, rather than egocentric speech becoming social, as Piaget would say, Vygotsky would argue that social speech becomes egocentric before being internalized as thought. For example, when Harry is 3 years 6 months and at our house, he reacts nervously when he hears a sudden noise. Harry: *"What was that noise?"* Me: *"It must be our next door neighbour"*. Harry seems to internalize this idea when he hypothesizes, *"If you hear some noise, it just be me"*. Harry is obviously thinking that *if* he can hear the neighbour, *then* people can hear him and he externalizes his thought by hypothesizing about other people hearing him make a noise (Diaz *et al.* 1990: 134).

2 Zone of proximal development

A second theory put forward by Vygotsky is also connected to Harry's interactions with other people. Vygotsky would argue that what Harry achieves today with assistance from others, he will achieve tomorrow alone (Moll 1990). Vygotsky is interested in using Harry's 'strengths' to help him learn more (Vygotsky 1986: 189). Rather than focusing on what Harry cannot do, Vygotsky focuses on what Harry can nearly do alone. Vygotsky calls this Harry's 'zone of proximal development'. In Vygotsky's view, Harry does not simply imitate what an adult or more capable peer models, but 'the adult– child dyad engages in joint problem-solving, where both share knowledge and responsibility for the task' (Diaz *et al.* 1990: 140). An example of this kind of collaboration is when Harry (aged 3 years 4 months) is interested in constructing a marble run at nursery. He and Lorna, his Family Worker, tackle the problem together. Each offers suggestions about how to connect the run so that marbles run across and down each rung. They try their ideas out and test whether the run works by placing marbles at the top and observing what happens. Harry is involved in constructing the marble run with adults and older children on many occasions before he constructs it alone. It appears important that when Harry and Lorna work together, he is involved in exploring and trying out ideas and not simply watching. Also, it is Harry who is highly motivated to construct the run. He is excited and gives the task his undivided attention.

3 Children develop spontaneous or everyday concepts before learning scientific concepts

Vygotsky would argue that Harry develops spontaneous or everyday concepts through his early experiences and explorations. Harry is not consciously using these concepts. They are second nature to him. On the other hand, Harry is taught some scientific concepts, which begin with instructions. If Harry follows a set of instructions, he is consciously carrying out a set of procedures to reach a goal. This goal may not be a product.

Dweck and Leggett (1988) differentiate between 'performance goals' and 'learning goals'. Performance goals do involve an end point or product and therefore success or failure. Learning goals are open-ended and are about learning more about an aspect of the world. Dweck and Leggett find that children, who have learning goals rather than performance goals, are more likely to persist and to achieve mastery.

Vygotsky (1986: 172) says that when Harry learns 'scientific concepts' by being taught, this causes him to remodel his earlier spontaneous concepts. Harry uses his earlier everyday concepts to mediate his newly acquired scientific concepts (Vygotsky 1986: 161). So, both kinds of concepts influence each other within Harry. Spontaneous or everyday concepts begin in the concrete and become more abstract. Scientific concepts begin in the abstract and become more concrete (Vygotsky 1986: xxxiv). Vygotsky (1986) says that 'The development of a spontaneous concept must have reached a certain level for the child to be able to absorb a related scientific concept' (p. 194). Vygotsky uses the example of 'historical concepts', which can only 'begin to develop when the child's everyday concept of the past is sufficiently differentiated – when his own life and the life of those around him can be fitted into the elementary generalization "in the past and now". . .'.

Often we see Harry puzzled or not quite understanding the process of time passing and change. For example, Harry (aged 2 years 8 months) expresses his idea that "*Uncle Paul has two cats*". Harry has seen Jasper the kitten and Jasper the cat. Harry's parents explain that the kitten has grown up. They find it difficult to convince Harry that the kitten and cat are one and the same. Vygotsky would say that Harry's everyday concept and experience of time passing and growth is not sufficiently developed yet to be able to take on the abstract concepts of time passing and growth. Harry is using his experiences of seeing a kitten, then a cat. He comes up with the logical idea that *"Uncle Paul must have two cats"*. His parents, however, are offering him the scientific concept that time passes and changes occur. Harry is not ready to absorb this idea until his everyday knowledge includes some experiences of seeing for himself how time and growth relate. (We will see further evidence of Harry's growing knowledge in this area in Chapter 8.)

John Bowlby

John Bowlby is born in 1907. Like Piaget and Vygotsky, Bowlby seems to be strongly influenced by his early experiences within his own family. His brother, Tony, only 13 months older than John, is his mother's clear favourite. The children are raised mostly by nurses (Holmes 1993). John's nurse is responsive and is said to be the only one among the staff to play with the children (John Bowlby Conference, 2001). At the beginning of the First World War, John (aged 7) and his brother are sent away to boarding school. We can only speculate about the pain this separation may have caused him. As a young man, before going to medical school, John gets a job in a 'progressive school for maladjusted children'. He finds he can communicate with the disturbed children, 'whose difficulties seem to be related to their unhappy and disrupted childhood' (Holmes 1993: 18). Bowlby spends many years formulating his theories.

Bowlby's major ideas

1   Human beings have an inbuilt need to maintain proximity to a caregiver. He calls this 'attachment behaviour'. The function of attachment behaviour is protection from predators.
2   Children use responsive adults as a secure base from which to explore.
3   Children build up internal working models of how they expect adults to respond to them, based on their experiences of early interactions with their caregivers.

1 Children display attachment behaviour
Bowlby would say that Harry has a biological need to stay near the adults who care for him. Bowlby compares the behaviour of young animals with the behaviour of young humans. Bowlby would argue

that Harry bonds with his caregivers during the early months and years of his life. At first Bowlby (1953) thinks that Harry needs to experience 'a warm, intimate and continuous relationship with his mother (or permanent mother-substitute – one person who stead-fastly 'mothers' him) in which both find satisfaction and enjoyment' (p. 13). Bowlby formulates his theories during the 1950s, shortly after the disruptions of the war and based on a group of dysfunctional adolescents. The idea that children need **one** continuous relationship has since been adapted. It is now thought that Harry forms attach-ments with several people. He may prefer one to another, but when he is separated from his main caregiver, he plays quite happily if another of his attachment figures is present. We see, in Chapter 1, that Harry (aged 1 year 5 months) is not happy when I am babysitting. He begins to play only when his Grandpop arrives and cuddles him. Is Harry exerting his power over a situation? Is he clearly showing his preference for his Grandpop? Does he need two people to feel safe?

When Harry attends crèche, it is important for him to have a key worker, someone who will always greet him, feed him, change his nappy and play with him. The 'key worker' is always the same person and this helps Harry to feel secure when he is in crèche and not near his parents or main carers (QCA 2000).

When Harry is 3 years old, his parents separate. For some months, Harry expresses his loss and grief by becoming distressed and clingy. He clings so as to stay close to the important adults in his world. The separation and sense of loss threatens the security and predictability of Harry's world. Harry seems to have some understanding that his life will never be the same again. (We will explore how Harry and his family adapt to their new situation later in the book.)

2 Children need a 'secure base' from which to explore
Bowlby would say that the responsive adults in Harry's world enable him to feel secure. Harry knows that his parents or carers will respond when he needs to be close to them. These adults provide a secure base from which to explore. Harry can be curious and move away from his parents or carers in the secure knowledge that they will respond if he calls out or cries. He trusts that they will keep him safe. This secure base enables Harry to become involved for relatively long periods in investigating the properties of materials, in problem-solving and in creating play with objects and other people. If Harry's attachment were insecure, he would probably be using up a great deal of his

energy in trying to maintain proximity to his caregiver and to seek comfort. In this situation, Harry would not feel free to explore. Goldberg (2000) says, 'Main (1991) suggests that from infancy onward throughout life, insecure individuals must deploy some of their limited resources in monitoring the availability of attachment figures and engaging strategies to recruit and maintain their attention' (p. 156).

Harry stays closer to his parents in a new environment or situation or when he experiences anything as threatening. For example, at Christmas, when Harry is 1 year 7 months, his dad takes Harry and Georgia to the town centre to see the Christmas lights being switched on. Harry appears scared and needs reassurance when he gets close to Santa.

3 Children build up internal working models

Bowlby would say that Harry gradually 'builds up a set of models' of himself and others 'based on repeated patterns of interactive experience' (Holmes 1993: 78). Harry clearly expects adults to respond to his needs and to him. We see how he expresses his fear of Santa and how adults respond. They listen to his fears and stay close and reassure him. They try to convey messages like "*We are here to protect you*" and "*We have seen Santa before and he won't hurt you*". Harry is affected by his history of experiences of other people. If many of his experiences are of reliable adults, who react to him in the same way each time he comes into contact with them, then he learns to expect a positive reaction, encouragement and protection. Another reaction from adults might be consistently negative, discouraging and threatening. In this case, Harry would build a very different model of expectations. A third way of adults reacting to Harry might be inconsistent, sometimes responsive, at other times unresponsive or threatening. In this situation, Harry would not know what to expect and would be 'disorganized' and 'preoccupied' in trying to ascertain the mood or reaction of the adults.

Contemporary theories that help us understand Harry's development and learning

Many contemporary educationalists are drawing on the theories of Piaget, Vygotsky, Bowlby and other great psychologists and educationalists when formulating their theories about how children learn.

The concept of 'involvement'

Professor Ferre Laevers draws on Piaget's theory about 'fundamental schemes' or patterns that children explore and Vygotsky's theory about 'the zone of proximal development' when thinking about Harry's process of learning (Laevers 1993, 1994). Laevers proposes that we can assess when Harry is engaged in 'deep level learning' by noticing the 'involvement signals' that Harry displays (Laevers 1997). Laevers suggests that Harry is using his 'exploratory drive' when he displays several of the following signals:

- concentration
- energy
- complexity and creativity
- expression and posture
- persistence
- accuracy
- reaction time
- language
- satisfaction

When Harry displays these signals, he is intrinsically motivated and challenged. He is accommodating new patterns to his current model and is at the edge of his capability.

Laevers also outlines a scale of involvement, going from 1 (uninvolved) to 5 (deeply involved and not to be distracted). It would be impossible for Harry to be deeply involved all of his time, but if he is never deeply involved, then we are not providing an adequate curriculum for him. We are judging our provision *not* Harry's ability.

The concept of 'well-being'

Laevers says that when considering Harry's process of learning, we must assess his 'involvement' *and* his 'well-being' (Laevers 1997). If Harry's level of well-being is low, then he will find it hard to relax and to become involved. Laevers suggests signals of well-being are:

- openness and receptivity
- flexibility
- self-confidence and self-esteem
- being able to defend oneself and assertiveness
- vitality
- relaxation and inner peace
- enjoyment without restraints
- being in close contact with one's inner self (Laevers 1997: 18–19)

If we find that Harry's well-being is low, then we can discuss the possible causes with his parents and make plans to help Harry. For example, when Harry's parents separate, his Family Worker at nursery can make it possible for him to express his feelings about living in two houses. Lorna might encourage Harry to talk by telling him a story about a child whose parents live separately, or she might sit alongside him when he is playing with play people at the doll's house to discover and to help him express his feelings. As practitioners, we need to be sensitive to his parents' raw feelings about their recent separation. We can help by working with Harry's parents to reassure him that he is loved.

The concept of schemas

During the 1970s, Chris Athey shared information with parents about schemas:

> Schemas are patterns of repeatable actions that lead to early categories and then to logical classifications. As a result of applying a range of action schemas to objects, infants arrive at the generalizations that objects are 'throwable', 'suckable' and 'bangable'.
>
> (Athey 1990: 36)

Harry's parents both attend sessions about schemas, when he starts nursery. This gives them some new language for describing Harry's actions, and a means with which they can have a meaningful dialogue with his workers at nursery. They notice that Harry is a strong 'connector'. This helps his parents to provide resources at home for Harry to connect, as well as providing a focus for communi-cating with Lorna and other workers.

Learning styles

Howard Gardner (1991), like Loris Malaguzzi in Reggio Emilia, believes that children learn in many different ways. Gardner argues that if children learn in different ways, then we should take into account each child's learning style when we are teaching. It is helpful to consider whether Harry learns through:

- language
- logical-mathematical analysis
- spatial representation
- an understanding of himself
- musical thinking
- the use of the body to solve problems or to make things
- an understanding of others

Harry may favour one style over another. Our aim is to offer a rich environment at nursery and at home in which there is scope to use many ways of learning about the world. The approach is a broad one, so that there is a familiar 'way in' for each child as well as the freedom and support to discover new ways of learning. For example, when Harry starts nursery, he mainly uses 'spatial representation' and 'his body to solve problems'. He continues to use his whole body, but in new ways and with new equipment, such as pulleys to lift weights. He also has available to him at nursery, musical instruments, new people to get to know, computers and all sorts of writing materials, as well as clay, paint, cornflour and other messy materials to explore.

Learning dispositions

Katz and Chard (1989: 35) introduce the idea of 'dispositions' or 'habits of mind' being important. They say that educators and parents

> ... readily nominate many dispositions when asked to indicate their hopes for the outcome of education. They gen-erally agree on the desirability of encouraging children's

curiosity, creativity, resourcefulness, independence, initia-
tive, responsibility and other positive dispositions.

(Katz and Chard 1989: 30)

These are ways of being that are helpful to children when they are
learning. Katz and Chard suggest that 'some approaches to teaching
knowledge and skills may possibly undermine the disposition to use
them' (p. 30). They are concerned that 'formal academic or direct
instruction in the early years may jeopardise the development of
desirable dispositions' (p. 30).

Carr (2001: 23), in describing the New Zealand curriculum, Te
Whariki, talks about 'Five domains of learning dispositions'. She
describes the domains of dispositions as

- taking an interest
- being involved
- persisting with difficulty or uncertainty
- communicating with others
- taking responsibility

Rather than a learning disposition being viewed as 'the possession
of an individual, like temperament', something that you either have
or do not have, Carr (2001) views a learning disposition as 'situated
in and interwoven with action and activity' (p. 47). We can foster
the inclination to behave in one way, rather than another way. So,
when we set up the environment as a workshop to be explored, we are
encouraging Harry's curiosity and independence.

Analysing narrative observations of Harry

The first time Harry (aged 3 years 5 months) is the target of our observation at nursery, five written narrative observations are made of
Harry's play. This is one of them:

> 'Harry came outside carrying his snack tag (a ticket with his
> name on and an elastic loop to hang up in the snack area). He
> hung it on the handlebars of the large yellow bike and rode
> around outside with his tag dangling. Harry then found the large
> yellow trailer, which goes with the bike. Harry carefully reversed

the bike and attached the trailer to the back of the bike. This took a lot of struggling and patience. A few minutes later, he disconnected the trailer and walked up the slide, sliding down on his belly. Harry ran up the slide, balancing at the top of the slope and saying "Look at me! Look at me!" He went indoors to tell his mummy something. He came out again and ran up the slide and down again carrying his snack tag, then took the tag inside. Harry returned holding a brush in the air, then sweeping it along the ground. He said "Look at me, me got brush!" Harry used the brush to sweep up and down the slide. Then he pushed the brush over the top of the slide, letting it fall down the steps to the ground. He lay down headfirst on his front to retrieve the brush and to pull it back up, over the top and down the slide. He repeated this several times. He said "Look at me, look at me you big bumble bee".

(Harry was observed for 30 minutes)'

We need to use theories to analyse the observation so that we can try to work out where Harry is in his learning, what he might be trying to learn and which actions are important to him.

The above observation provides some important clues about Harry's vital interests:

- Harry carries his snack tag, then a brush from indoors to out. He experiments with carrying them in different ways, for example, *'hanging the tag'* on the handlebars of a bike and *'holding the brush in the air'*. The carrying or *'transporting'* of objects in different ways seems to be of interest to Harry (Athey 1990: 89).
- Harry is learning kinaesthetically (through his body) to feel the differences, for example, when carrying the *'brush in the air'* and sliding down the slide *'on his belly'*. Harry is using his body to make discoveries about objects in his environment.
- Harry *'struggles'* to attach a trailer to the back of a bike. A few minutes later he *'disconnects'* it and does something different. This indicates that Harry is interested in the process of *'connecting'*, rather than the product, which is connected.
- Harry has a positive sense of himself, saying *"Look at me!"* several times. His well-being is high (Laevers 1997).

- When Harry *'retrieves the brush'*, he uses his body, as a line, to reach the brush. He repeats this several times, indicating that he is either *'practising'* or *'wallowing'* in his play (Bruce 1997).
- Harry extends his language, repeating "*Look at me*" and connecting a rhyming phrase towards the end of the play.
- Overall, Harry seems to be acting on objects to make things happen. He seems to be understanding 'functional dependency effects', as described by Athey (1990: 70). For example, reaching the brush is functionally dependent on Harry lying down and stretching towards the brush. This is not a random act on Harry's part. He is solving a problem, which he has created for himself.

At the weekly curriculum-planning meeting, Lorna reflects on and analyses the observations of Harry. We use a framework for analysis. We think about:

- how *'involved'* Harry is during the whole session (Laevers 1997);
- how his *'well-being'* is (Laevers 1997);
- which *'schemas'* or patterns Harry is exploring (Athey 1990; Bruce 1991; Arnold 1997, 1999);
- which areas of learning he is exploring (QCA 2000);
- his preferred learning style (Gardner 1991);
- who he plays with (Pollard 1996);
- his *'dispositions'* (Carr 2001); and
- how adults relate to Harry (Pascal and Bertram 1997; Whalley and Arnold 1997).

By discussing and analysing the observations of Harry, we begin to understand his personality and to get a sense of his deep interests. We make action plans to support and extend what Harry is doing. The first time Harry is observed in nursery, staff notice that he:

- is involved at level 3 indoors and level 4 out of doors (Laevers 1997);
- has a high level of well-being (Laevers 1997);
- is currently exploring *'trajectories'*, *'transporting'* and *'connection'* (Athey 1990);

- is covering personal, social and emotional development (*"Look at me!"*), mathematical development (*'increasing length by adding trailer to bike'* and *'using his body as a line to reach the brush'*), creative development (*'linking actions together – pulling brush up and down slide'* and *'making up a rhyme'*); physical development (*'riding'*, *'reversing'*, *'balancing'*, *'pushing'*), communication, language and literacy (*'making up a rhyme'*) and knowledge and understanding of the world (*'hanging loop on handlebars'*) (QCA 2000);
- uses his body to explore the environment (Gardner 1991);
- is making links with adults (Pollard 1996);
- is curious and uses humour (Bruce and Meggitt 1996; Carr 2001).

During their daily chats with Lorna, Harry's parents tell her that, at home, he is playing with string. He winds the string around handles, his cars and anything else he can find. This links with *'hanging his snack tag on the handlebars'* and *'attaching the trailer to the bike'*.

Making action plans to extend learning

The action plans that are made to extend Harry's learning are:

- To tell Harry the story of 'Papa, please get the moon for me' – this book contains an extending ladder, which staff think will appeal to Harry, because of his interest in trajectories and connecting.
- To make all of the Family Workers aware that Harry is making relationships with adults.
- To provide string and also to offer Harry a fishing game, magnets and electric circuits to build on his interest in connecting.

Harry takes up the opportunities to use the fishing game, magnets and electric circuits over a period of time. At home, he is trying to connect things together with string. At nursery, he plays with string and also learns about how magnets are attracted to each other and connect. These experiences help Harry to widen his ideas about the concept of 'connecting'.

Summary

In this chapter, we have been considering Harry's development and learning through the theoretical perspectives of Piaget, Vygotsky and Bowlby. We have also introduced the following contemporary theories, which can help us to interpret Harry's development and learning:

- involvement and well-being (Laevers 1994, 1997)
- schemas (Athey 1990)
- learning styles (Gardner 1991)
- dispositions to learn and learning dispositions (Katz and Chard 1989; Carr 2001)

Table 2.1   Schemas mentioned in Chapter 2

Trajectory containment
Lines
Going through a boundary
Connection
Transporting

We have looked at making and analysing narrative observations. In Chapter 3, we will consider Harry's physical development.

3 Harry's physical development

We begin by considering how Harry gains control of his own body, learns to handle tools skilfully and becomes aware of himself in relation to other people. It is the most obvious area of development in young children and also the most important. Physical activity is not simply an outlet for excess energy, but lays the foundation for thought. When we are learning to move, we are also learning to think. Dewey (1998: 206) states that:

> The joy the child shows in learning to use his limbs, to translate what he sees into what he handles, to connect sounds with sights, sights with taste and touch, and the rapidity with which intelligence grows in the first year and a half . . . are sufficient evidence that the development of physical control is not a physical, but an intellectual achievement.

Nathan Isaacs (1966) tells us that 'Thought is in fact for Piaget just action carried on inwardly' (p. 9). More recently, Davies (1995) reminds us that 'many people find "moving and thinking" and "moving and feeling" less familiar and accessible notions' and that 'these ideas . . . remain unexplored and untested' (p. 49). These are complex ideas, which few researchers feel able to tackle. While we value highly the marks made when Harry moves a pencil or other tool across some paper, we rarely give enough attention to the actions that precede the making of a mark. Davies (1995) states that 'information concerning cognitive development appears in movement, where children use their bodies as a major framework of reference, before other more established contexts' (p. 49). We often see Harry try out things with his whole body in an attempt to understand. As parents and educators, we can encourage this physical trying out and will be more likely to if we can see the benefits for Harry.

This chapter is divided into the following sections:

- Harry uses his whole body and manipulates objects to explore his world
- Learning to handle tools
- Becoming aware of himself in relation to other people

Harry uses his whole body and manipulates objects to explore his world

Harry explores up/down movements

At 1 year 1 month, Harry is at our house. The kitchen stepladder is outside the back door.

> 'Harry holds onto the step ladder with two hands, puts his left foot on the bottom step, then struggles to bring his right foot alongside it. Grandpop puts his hand behind and near to Harry's bottom. Then Harry puts his right foot on the next step. He holds on to the sides of the top of the stool and uses his left knee on the second step and then on top to lever his body on to the top of the stool. Grandpop lifts him around so that he is facing the camera. Harry puts both hands between his legs and beams towards the camera. Then he rocks forward and back. Grandpop puts his hand behind Harry's back. Harry feels Grandpop's hand and leans right back. Grandpop says "You'll fall", then holds both of Harry's hands and helps him to jump down'. (video clip)

As an observer, two things strike me about this clip: (1) the obvious danger if Harry were to fall and (2) his belief and trust that he can try anything. As early years educators, we are taught to trust children to go as far as they think they can. This usually works, as children will try out each movement as Harry does here. We cannot know how Harry would have got on without an adult nearby. Unless we allow Harry to try, he will not learn. We could remove the ladder and therefore the risk of falling, but how would Harry learn to climb without real opportunities?

Making links with Harry's cognitive development

When climbing the stepladder, Harry is learning about 'up' and 'down'. When he reaches the top, he is 'on top' and can survey the world from a new position. Athey (1990) describes 'dynamic vertical schemas' in terms of 'four different stage levels: motor, symbolic representation, functional dependency and "thought" ' (p. 131). She argues that there is 'continuity from stage to stage'. In other words, Harry explores up/down movements at a motor level first. The feedback he receives is through his senses. He experiences the struggle and effort climbing up takes, how it feels when he gets to the top and can sit down. It is an emotional experience too for Harry. It is no coincidence that he *'beams'*. He is showing satisfaction and pleasure. In Harry's brain, the experience of climbing is linked with success and pleasure. This motivates him to repeat his actions and to look for other challenges. The physical skill he gains is almost incidental.

Although motor level is the first stage of learning about up/down for Harry, it is a way of exploring and discovering that he continues to use throughout his life. It becomes part of his repertoire. It also enables Harry to move on and use up/down at a symbolic and functional level.

When Harry is 3 years old, he and Georgia are playing in the garden:

> *'Harry and Georgia were playing a game with James and Stacey (next door neighbours) – throwing things over the fence and then James and Stacey throwing them back. It began with a ball. Harry threw skittles, a plastic cup and a plastic pan over. Harry was standing on a chair or on top of the slide to do this. He was very excited and animated'.*

We are not sure how the game began. It certainly becomes intentional at some point. It seems that Harry discovers that it is easier to get the object to go over the fence from an elevated position. He is also learning about how to move his body to throw a particular height and distance. So Harry is using the up/down schema at a *functional depend-*

ency level. The object going over the fence is functionally dependent on the power and angle of the throw.

One week later: *'Harry and Georgia are throwing small, plastic balls onto the roof of the lean-to and giggling as the balls roll to the edge and fall back down'*. Here Harry is combining the ideas of 'up/down' and 'on top'. The roof slopes and Georgia and Harry find it very funny that the balls roll down and off each time. Again the ball reaching the roof is *functionally dependent* on the power and angle of the throw.

When Harry is 4 years 6 months, he is still thinking about and exploring ideas about 'up/down' and 'on top'. He has been at school for 2 months.

> *'Harry came to meet me at work tonight – everything related to vertical trajectories – he jumped up high, called himself 'Jumping Jim'. He carried the long window pole and lifted it above his head (like a weightlifter lifting weights). He spoke about who was big and who was little. In the car he said his teacher had been "horrible" to him and to Thomas. He said he wasn't the "bestest" in his class. (Later on I reminded him that he was the "bestest" when he had his Achievement Assembly.)'*

Here Harry is using ideas about 'up/down' and 'on top' at different levels. He is experiencing up/down at the *motor level* when he jumps. When he calls himself 'Jumping Jim', he refers to the action of jumping but is using the idea of a person who jumps *as a symbol* to communicate the idea. This also links to the Letterland alphabet symbols that Harry's school is using to teach phonics. Harry is experimenting with how to carry the very long window pole. Keeping the pole horizontal and balancing the weight evenly is *functionally dependent* on Harry raising both arms in the air. He is using size at a *thought level* when he talks about who is big and who is little. In the conversation about his teacher, he is using the concept of *"being the bestest"*, which relates to being 'on top' of the class or at the top of a vertical trajectory. Harry shows that he can *think about* himself going up or down in his teacher's estimation.

Harry explores vertical to horizontal movements

No sooner is Harry walking and running confidently than he begins to experiment with moving his body in different ways. At 1 year

7 months: '*Saw Harry trying to do handstands outside the family room when Georgia and Steph were doing handstands. He managed to place his hands on the floor but could not lift his feet off the floor*'. A week later: '*Harry stands on a low chair and jumps – his feet barely leave the surface but he falls off*'. At 1 year 8 months and still wearing his nappy: '*Harry came to the toilet with Georgia and me. He pulled off pieces of toilet roll and bent forward "to wipe his bottom"*'.

None of these movements appear significant until we notice Harry (aged 1 year 9 months) manipulate the playmobil bin lids, connecting them to the bins and then opening and shutting them (horizontal to vertical movements). '*He gives them to me to fix . . . he tries to shut the lids . . . then he manipulates the bins for a while opening and shutting the lids*'. Five days later: '*Harry lined all the bins up with the lids open*'. At 1 year 10 months: '*Harry brought four play people with him. He bent each play person's legs and lay each one down on the floor in turn. He then straightened each set of legs and again lay them down in turn. (Vertical to horizontal movement?)*' At 1 year 11 months:

> '*Harry tried to copy Georgia doing a handstand. He leaned forward resting his head and both hands on the floor without raising his feet off the floor. When Georgia did a handstand by putting her hands on the couch, he fetched a small chair, placed it next to the couch, then stood on it and threw himself forward onto the couch*'.

Harry seems to be trying to move his body through 180 degrees.

At 2 years 1 month: '*Harry pushed his bike over and said "Over!" Also made a bridge with his body (Colette says he often does this)*'. That summer, when Harry is 2 years 3 months: '*put gravel in the large metal watering can and tipped it out*'.

A toy that Harry plays with over a long period of time (from when he is 2 years until he is 7 years) is a Dinky transporter with cars. He remembers that he particularly enjoyed manipulating the ramp, which, when closed, becomes a tail gate. He would lie down on the floor and study how it closes. In this instance, he is studying how the ramp goes from a horizontal to a vertical position.

His investigations increase in complexity. At 3 years 1 month, Harry is in the garden with his mum: '*Harry wants to fold the garden chair. Colette shows him how. He nods and says "Ah-like that!"*' Has he been hypothesizing about *how* it folds up?

Figure 3.1 Harry's first day at nursery.

On his first day at nursery, aged 3 years 3 months: '*Harry plays in the sand with a digger*'. Here he practises using a set of procedures that involve horizontal to vertical and back to horizontal movements. He uses a lever to operate the arm of the digger and also to operate the scoop. Harry is coordinating a number of movements.

Harry continues working on understanding vertical to horizontal movements for a long time. He uses his own body, a variety of objects and, eventually, he represents some of his ideas by drawing. His investigations appear to be about movement and positioning, for example, when he moves golf clubs and makes a '*cross*' (see Chapter 7 for the full observation). At 5 years 7 months, he draws a 'Lucy Lamplady' (letter L) upright and on its side. At 6 years 7 months, Harry draws a castle with a moat. He says, "*The bridge is down*".

Athey (1990) points out that babies and young children perceive and then represent vertical and horizontal before oblique. She says, 'For instance, children can copy vertical and horizontal lines before they can copy oblique lines' (p. 94). Athey also acknowledges that physical movement (e.g. sliding down a slope) contributes to the ability to draw oblique lines. So when Harry slides down a slide, it heightens his perception of the oblique position.

Figure 3.2 A castle with a moat: 'The bridge is down'.

Harry learns to handle tools

Although Harry does not often choose to write or draw, as a young child he frequently uses tools as extensions of his arms and, in doing so, becomes an expert. He is curious about how things work and this curiosity leads him to gain a great deal of experience in manipulating objects. At 1 year 6 months: *'First he wanted to use keys with the lock (front door, back door and even washing machine)'*. A week later, on the train to London: *'Harry posted coins behind the seat on the train'*. Another week later, on Christmas Day, when Harry is 1 year 7 months: *'Used key – was pleased when key stayed in crack of door. Tried key on food. Slipped counters under door'*. Harry seems to be trying to work out *how* a key unlocks a door or perhaps what happens when small objects disappear.

At Harry's home, the children have a table in the corner of the living-room with writing and drawing materials and scissors. By the time Harry is 2 years 1 month, *'He can cut out one-handed holding the paper in his other hand'*. Harry creates many opportunities to prac-tise his skills. At 2 years 3 months: *'Colette and the children came around for a barbecue. Harry chose to try to eat with a long, plastic salad spoon. He also loved using the tongs to carry sausage from a serving dish to his plate (this took a lot of concentration)'*. At 2 years 11 months, Harry tries to hit a ball with a golf club for the first time: *'He found it quite difficult to connect the club with the ball. He liked leaning the club against a post or chair'*. Maybe, at this stage, Harry is more interested in the oblique position than in using the club to hit a ball.

When Harry is 2 years 11 months, he does his first emergent writing. He moves the pen in a zig zag across the paper. Browne (1999) says that this sort of 'joined up scribble . . . shows a child's appreci-ation of the recurring principle of writing' (p. 90). Harry knows that symbols are used repeatedly. The diary says *'Harry did this writing, held it up and said "Ha-rry-a-poo"'*. Georgia is now in her first year at school. Is her sounding out words influencing Harry?

At 3 years of age Harry is filmed in the garden. Now, he finds a way of hitting a ball with a golf club: *'Harry puts the end of the golf club against the ball and pushes it to make it move'*.

Harry continues to find physical challenges. He begins to use the computer at our house and at nursery when he starts attending at 3 years 3 months. He is observed using a pump action container

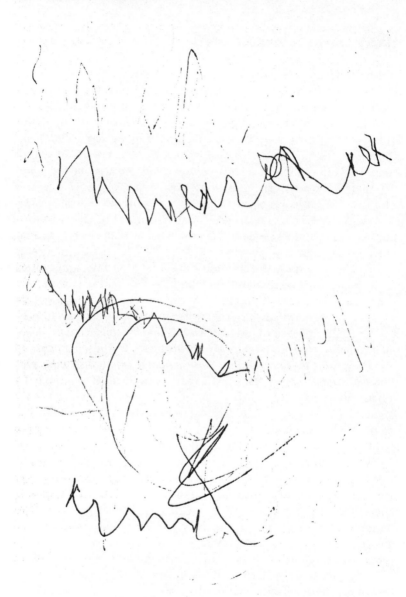

Figure 3.3 Harry's first emergent writing.

Figure 3.4 Harry carrying Maureen's long pincers.

(aged 3 years 3 months) and a plant sprayer (aged 3 years 4 months). His favourite challenge, however, and one he always takes up, is using the long pincers that Maureen, our cleaner at nursery, uses to pick up toys dropped behind radiators or to reach inaccessible corners. They are about 5 feet long and the pincers close and open when you squeeze the handle. Harry is only allowed to use them when he visits nursery after the other children have gone home. The first record of Harry using the pincers is when he is 3 years 8 months: *'Harry used Maureen's long pincers to pick up string and move it'*. This is no mean feat.

Harry frequently manipulates string at home and at nursery (see Chapters 4 and 7 for fuller descriptions of his use of string). Harry continues to seek out physical challenges. At nursery Harry is observed:

- hammering nails into a tree trunk (aged 3 years 6 months);
- using a hand drill (aged 3 years 6 months);
- hammering broad and narrow nails into wood in a precise formation (aged 3 years 8 months);
- mopping the floor with a large mop (aged 3 years 8 months);
- asking an adult to tie string around a loose branch, then dragging it around the outdoor area (aged 3 years 11 months);
- using a piece of guttering about 4 feet long to represent a gun (aged 4 years);
- pulling a piece of wood along behind a bike (the wood is connected to the back of the bike with string and trails on the ground) (aged 4 years);
- using a puppet (aged 4 years).

When Harry is 4 years 11 months, he goes to the Science Museum in London with the family. Here he demonstrates highly developed hand/eye coordination when using a hand-operated robot grabber. He is more skilled than his 6-year-old sister, mother and grandmother. Might that be a gender divide or purely the amount of first-hand experience and practice that Harry has had? Two days after the trip to the Science Museum, he asks for Maureen's *'grabber'* when he comes to nursery after school.

The following Christmas, when Harry is 5 years 7 months, he decorates a Christmas cake using coloured icing in tubes. He is in the kitchen alone while the family are watching television. He writes *'Merry Christmas Have Fun'* on the cake. Again, he does this skilfully with precision. The words are recognizable. He realizes that the icing has to be put on quite quickly as it is runny and will easily disinte-

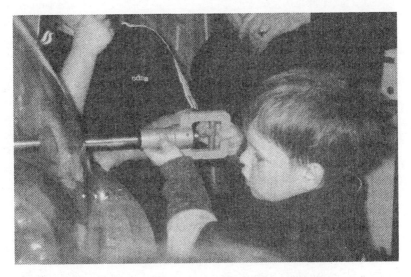

Figure 3.5 Harry using a hand-operated grabber at the Science Museum.

grate. Here he achieves something that many adults would find difficult.

What we have learned through observing Harry handling tools

Two things strike me about Harry's explorations with tools: (1) his persistence and (2) his choice of tools. Carr (2001) names 'persisting with difficulty or challenge' as one 'domain of disposition' (p. 24). She goes on to describe 'three parts' of the domain, the first of which is 'being ready' – 'enthusiasm for persisting with difficulty'. Harry certainly seems to have an enthusiasm for choosing to use tools that take a great deal of skill and practice. He is frequently likely to experience failure in using them. However, in Chapter 2 we hear about 'performance goals' and 'learning goals' (Dweck and Leggett 1988) and it is likely that Harry is developing 'learning goals'. He genuinely wants to know how the tools work and he is prepared to practise using them to find out. He is not being given an adult-directed task to accomplish. He is learning to use his own judgement both in choosing what to use and in how to use what he chooses. He sees himself as 'someone who persists with difficulty'.

The second part of a learning disposition, according to Carr (2001) is 'being willing'. She describes this as 'sensitivity to places and occasions in which it is worthwhile to tackle difficulty or uncertainty and to resist the routine' (p. 24). When Harry starts attending nursery, he is in the position of already knowing the building and some of the people. The nursery is set up as a workshop for children to explore. This appears to fit with Harry's natural way of learning. He seems willing, both in his home environments and at nursery, to persist. Of course, there are routines at nursery, like family grouptime, when Lorna gathers her group of children for stories, songs and conversations, but this is held towards the end of the session and is a time to both build and reflect on what children have been doing.

The third part of a learning disposition is 'being able', which Carr describes as 'problem-solving and problem-finding knowledge and skills; experience of making mistakes as part of solving a problem' (p. 24). This aspect focuses on Harry's ability to find and solve problems and to make mistakes. In his self-initiated explorations, Harry appears intrigued by particular aspects of the environment and seems able to create situations in which he can explore and discover things for himself.

Harry's choices of tools and materials to explore are certainly different to those his sister most frequently uses, for example, 'Georgia is motivated to make marks . . .' from 2 years old (Arnold 1999: 39). Harry focuses much more frequently on arranging and exploring objects and on making things happen. It is important to recognize, however, that Harry seeks out and persists with objects and materials that enable him to develop the fine motor skills that are required for writing. The current 'achievement gap' between boys and girls is put down to the fact that 'girls develop fine motor skills earlier, and are better equipped for the start of formal schooling . . . Boys tend to be more action-oriented – impatient, imaginative, inclined to take risks' (*Times Educational Supplement*, 15 November 2002). Perhaps we are not sufficiently tuned in to providing the resources that boys need to use to develop their skills. Early childhood practitioners, who are mostly women, often do not value boys' more active play. Holland (1999) describes how the lifting of a ban on guns, swords and super-hero play resulted in children extending their role play scenarios and in moving 'beyond imitation into the realms of imagination' (p. 5). Many early childhood settings ban guns when pulling triggers might actually contribute to those fine motor skills. I am not suggesting complete freedom without boundaries, but more close observation of what boys are doing and learning naturally.

Harry becomes aware of himself in relation to other people

In this chapter so far, we have been focusing on how Harry develops and coordinates his movements and skills as an individual. Another aspect of Harry's physical development is how he learns to coordinate his movements with the movements of other people. The records show that when Harry is 9 months old and sitting up, *'Harry plays "Row, row, row your boat" holding hands and rocking back and forth and making sounds (with a tuneful intonation)'*. Note that Harry is learning sounds and language alongside movements and that this is another aspect of physical development. Gopnik *et al.* (1998) state: 'The six- to twelve-month span appears to be the critical time for sound organization' (p. 108). Research has shown that babies become tuned into the languages spoken around them and after about 12 months become specialists in those languages.

As the second child in the family, Harry has always had Georgia around and often imitates the games she and the older children play, without completely understanding:

> *'It is Georgia's 5th birthday. Harry is 2 years 8 months. He mostly watches and does not join in the party games. When most of the other children have gone home, he takes all of his clothes off and initiates a game of hide and seek with Georgia and her friend Samantha (who lives in the close). Georgia covers her eyes and says ". . . 17, 18, 19, ready?" One second later Harry shouts, "Behind the curtain!" The two girls go and find Harry tangled up between the curtain and lining. It's Harry's turn to be 'on'. He puts his head on the couch and shouts "Ready?" "No – we're not ready yet". A few seconds later Harry gets up and runs and looks behind each curtain. Then he runs behind the couch and finally finds the two girls in the hall cupboard'. (video clip)*

What is interesting about this clip is that Harry chooses not to join in with several older children but, as soon as they leave, initiates a game with Georgia and Sam. He often takes all of his clothes off indoors. This seems to be about feeling comfortable.

He has a partial understanding of the game, but at this stage expects the others to use the same hiding place as him. The joy, for Harry, is being found, so he immediately tells them where he is. Harry does not quite understand that the hiding place can change each time. He understands that the girls are still in the room even though he cannot see them. Athey (1990: 38) would call this 'permanence of the object' as in 'peek-a-boo'. Harry can *think about* the two girls occupying the space he was in but he has not had enough experience to think about them occupying a different space in the room.

When Harry starts nursery, he plays alone or with an adult at first. He usually settles in the construction area with the trainset or mobilo. He often joins or is joined by other children with similar interests. The records show that several months after starting nursery, when Harry is 3 years 11 months, he starts playing regularly with Adam, who is 7 months older than him. They are part of a group of older children who enjoy playing chasing games. Often they use characters from videos to develop shared narratives. Themes such as 'Fireman Sam' or '101 Dalmatians' give the children shared content and characters as starting points for developing their own negotiated storylines. Harry chooses to play with older children and this 'mirrors' his home environment, where he often plays with older children in the closes or friends of Georgia's who visit their homes. Pollard (1996) found that a child he studied chose a friend with whom he could 'mirror his relationship within the family' (p. 53). Popular culture, including videos, is increasingly being recognized as valuable material for engaging boys in the curriculum (Marsh and Hallet 1999; Pahl 1999; Pen Green Portfolios 2000). Pahl (1999) says, 'Allowing He-Man into the classroom encourages boys to create and develop their narratives' (p. 98). These themes honour children's interests and ways of learning. These play scenarios are important to Harry as, through play, he not only learns to negotiate the rules with others, but to experience a range of feelings from different perspectives (Barnes 1995).

Harry starts school at 4 years 4 months and he finds his first year at school fairly demanding. He gets tired, does not like sitting down for very long and enjoys playtime. For his fifth birthday celebration, he invites two school friends to come bowling with the family: '*The three boys are like jumping beans, constantly on the move and bursting with energy. It is hard to imagine them sitting down at all'*. During his second year at school, Harry becomes much more engaged and begins to explore themes introduced at school at home. He especially enjoys learning about the planets and light and dark. He begins writing and reading more fluently.

Summary

In this chapter, we have been thinking about:

- physical movement as the basis of thought;
- how Harry explores and gains control of his body;
- how Harry learns to manipulate objects and to use tools as extensions of his body;
- how Harry becomes aware of himself in relation to other people.

Table 3.1 Schemas mentioned in Chapter 3

Up/down trajectory
On top
Horizontal to vertical trajectory
Vertical to horizontal trajectory
Oblique position

In the next chapter, we will consider Harry's personal, social and emotional development.

4 Listening to Harry – Harry's personal, social and emotional development

> ... what kind of interpersonal world or worlds does the infant create?
>
> (Stern 1985: 3)

In this chapter, we are trying to build up a picture of the emotional world Harry creates for himself. The chapter is divided into sections:

- How Harry communicates his needs and preferences as a baby
- Harry's developing relationships with others
- How Harry copes with the separation of his parents
- How we help Harry rise to the challenge of moving house, starting nursery and developing new routines
- Strategies Harry develops for dealing with change and transitions

How Harry communicates his needs as a baby

As we see in Chapter 1, Harry is a very determined little boy. He is able, even as a baby, to communicate his needs and desires. His mum says, *"We did not set ourselves up to fail. We would only insist on something with Harry when it was absolutely necessary"*. She explains that it is *"better for everyone involved"* if they are not constantly getting into power struggles, which involve winning and losing. From Harry's point of view, this means that his parents respond to his needs and desires and only occasionally insist on him doing something for his own benefit.

As a baby, Harry has a special type of blanket, which he uses when he is tired and wants a breastfeed. This is a 'transitional object' as described by Winnicott (1988: 30). The blanket replaces his mother when she is not there. Harry's need to use his blanket is *"a strong need for him"* according to his parents. Harry, aged 8 years, tells his mum she can give his blanket to someone they know who is having a baby. His parents have never put any pressure on him not to use his blanket and, in fact, his blanket is currently *"folded up and used to cover a soft toy dog"*, which he sometimes takes with him when he is going to stay overnight with anyone outside of his immediate family. In this case, Harry is using his dog as an 'object of transition' (T. Bruce, personal communication). He carries it from home to wherever he is staying. It may be a comfort and reminder of home when he is elsewhere. It does not, however, replace his mother like the blanket does.

Harry uses his treasure basket from when he is 6 months old. He is encouraged to manipulate and discover how the different materials react (Goldschmied 1987). He seems from an early age to be interested in the functional aspects of objects (Athey 1990). The knowledge of cause and effect, which Harry builds up over time through his exploration of objects and how they work, may contribute to his sense of agency. Bruner (1990) describes 'agentivity' as 'actions directed towards goals' (p. 77). Harry is a little boy, who is listened to and who is encouraged to find out how objects in his world work. A consequence of this encouragement is that Harry sees himself as being able to make things happen.

As far as communicating his wishes is concerned, Harry's mum recalls that *"Georgia could always understand what he wanted to say"*. Harry's speech is unclear for quite a long time but he rarely gives up when trying to communicate. Daniel Stern talks about himself, aged 7 years, being 'at a pivotal age' when he knew an infant's *and* an adult's language and was 'bilingual' (Stern 1985: ix). Stern describes himself as a 'watcher' and 'reader of the nonverbal'. Georgia, like Stern, is a watcher and can pick up on body language and intonation in understanding Harry. She often takes on a kind of mediating role.

Harry's developing relationships with others

We have seen that Harry is attracted to and gains comfort from other males within his family and this extends to Marcus, a male family

Figure 4.1 Harry and Georgia in their new house.

worker, when he begins attending nursery. Bowlby quotes research by Grinker, in which he found that well-adjusted young men 'identified strongly' with their fathers or father figures (Bowlby 1998: 393). Bowlby concludes that this kind of 'identification' is important in 'becoming and remaining (mentally) healthy'.

Harry takes longer to accept some adults, so much so that Katey (Deputy Head of Centre) notices when he seems to accept her: '*Harry (aged 1 year 8 months) is becoming much more sociable and friendly towards adults. Katey says he must have decided she is OK as he has started handing things to her*'. At the same age, he is becoming interested in and attempts to say the names of important people: '*Harry smiled at me and came for a cuddle – seemed pleased to see me. Can say "Mum", "Dad", "Mop", "Pop", "Dorda" and intones "Batman" (raises one arm above his head at the same time*'. Harry's impression of Batman helps him to communicate what he means.

Harry (aged 1 year 8 months) appears to use gesture to make a comparison when he is given asthma treatment to be administered using a volumatic: '*After Harry had had a go with the volumatic and put it down, he raised his arm and waved it in front like an elephant's trunk*'. (*Did that mean "the volumatic reminds me of an elephant's trunk"?*) Soon after this, when Harry is 1 year 10 months, he pretends to be a baby: '*He crawled on all fours and said "baby" very clearly. (Sometimes he is the "mummy".) He got into the pram and again said "Baby" '.*

Susan Isaacs (1933) comments on the preoccupation young children have with 'family play': 'The family situation provides a pattern for the whole world of experience with children under four years of age' (p. 350). This may be the beginning of Harry becoming aware of his own history. Two days later, he recognizes Eloise (when she was aged 11) in a photo album (she is 21). He also points to a photo of Georgia, as a baby, and says *"Dorda"*.

Not all of Harry's interactions with others are positive. At 1 year 8 months he says: *"No . . . even when he means Yes"*. Another strategy is *'making a high-pitched scream if Liam or Natasha want anything he has got'*. (Liam and Natasha are slightly younger than Harry and also use the crèche and family room at the Family Centre.)

At almost 2 years, when his parents are working and I am looking after the two children, *'Harry chose to wear Georgia's doggy pyjamas. He wanted to wear Georgia's new sandals – she wouldn't let him. He put on Ian's deck shoes but did not wear them for long'*. This does not sound significant until we hear that Harry continues to wear articles of clothing belonging to important people. His dad says, *"Even now, he wears my T shirt to bed sometimes"*. Is he wearing clothing to feel close to someone who is important? Does he wear Georgia's pyjamas as a comfort?

From 2 to 3 years, Harry listens to lots of stories and frequently engages in role play. Although stories are not his main interest, he often listens to the stories that are told to Georgia. Harry has some favourites. The 'Little Fluffy Duckling' who leaves the pond and looks for a home elsewhere is an early favourite of his, which he listens to over and over again. Another firm favourite is 'The Tunnel', in which a girl follows her brother into the unknown. These favourite stories are clearly representing emotional ideas. We can only guess at Harry's understanding of these issues but, if he listens to the stories many times, then we can speculate that he must be gaining some understanding of the underlying ideas.

How Harry copes with the separation of his parents

When Harry is 2 years 8 months, his parents decide that they are going to separate. They tell Georgia (aged 5 years) and Harry, reassuring them that they both still love them very much. Harry's dad feels that, "*Until there was a physical separation, it didn't hit him*". However, the diary account indicates that things change gradually over several months. During the period between being told and actually moving out, Harry is a bit fearful at times and also reveals some of his anxieties while he is playing.

Two months after the children are first told of the plan to separate, Harry finds it unusual that the whole family are going somewhere together by car. He queries: "*Why we all go?*" Then, 3 weeks later, Harry mentions "*All of us*" and "*Our daddy*". Colette notes that she has not heard him use the pronoun 'our' before.

Around the same time, Harry (aged 2 years 10 months) is playing with Teddy Tom (a small teddy): '*Harry carried Tom carefully, saying "He's got no daddy", then "he's got no mummy" – "no brothers, no sisters". At the same time, Teddy Tim (a larger teddy) is the "fixing man" for the cars*'. Might Harry be expressing his fears about being abandoned and isolated through his play? Bowlby (1998) says, 'parental quarrels carry with them the risk that a parent may depart' (p. 249). Harry's parents do their best not to quarrel in front of the children during this difficult time. However, Harry's real fear may be that he will have '*no daddy*', '*no mummy*' or '*no sister*'. He has recently been expressing his understanding of the family as a whole unit through talking about '*all of us*'. No sooner is he able to think about '*all of us*' than he needs to deal with the idea of the individual people, who make up the family, as separate.

At around the same time, when Harry is 2 years 10 months, several changes occur. His mum begins working during the day rather than during the evening. This is in preparation for moving to her own house. Harry is cared for during the day by a number of people: his dad (who works mainly evenings), his grandad, his uncle Paul and a new childminder, Mags.

When Harry is 2 years 11 months, his dad goes away to Bournemouth for the weekend. Harry reacts by '*wearing Georgia's coat with the hood up*'. So, although Harry's parents have been trying to persuade him to wear a coat to keep him warm for almost 3 years and he has stubbornly resisted, he suddenly decides to wear Georgia's coat with the hood up. Is he communicating his distress by doing something out of character for him? Does wearing something of Georgia's comfort him? Does keeping the hood up mean 'I don't want to hear anything else'?

Just after his third birthday, Harry '*keeps frightening himself by talking about monsters*'. Is this a fear of his unknown future? Harris (1989) points out that 3-year-olds can become confused about reality and imagination. Might vulnerability and fear blur the boundaries between reality and fantasy? A week later, when I am visiting, Harry has two emotional outbursts:

> 'When his Gran has allowed him to take a couple of photos and he wants to continue and take more, she says "No". He throws his tap-it hammer across the room'.

> 'His mum asks both children to stop shouting and reaching up for money for ice cream. Harry bursts into tears and asks his Gran to go away'.

When Harry is 3 years 1 month, his mum finds the house that she decides to buy. Harry and his sister visit the house and meet the family who are living there. It is only two streets away from where the family are currently living. The family living in the new house have a dog. Harry begins to express his fear of dogs: 'Harry is looking serious and anxious. A dog barked in next door's garden and he cried. I reassured him that it could not get into our garden. He asked if it could jump over the fence. I said "No" '. When Harry's mum asks if he likes the new house, he says he does not like the dog. His mum again reassures him that 'the dog will move far, far away with the family when they move'.

Bowlby (1998) notes that there is 'a high incidence of fear of animals' in children of this age (p. 141). The accumulation of changes, fear of the future and a strange dog living in their new house, all seem to be too much for Harry. Is he able to imagine the house without the dog?

One night, when I am babysitting, Harry (aged 3 years 1 month) wakes up. He has wet the bed and is really distressed. I get him changed and cuddle him. He tells me he wants his mummy. He wants to tell her he hurt his toe at Grandad's. I promise to leave a note for mummy about his toe and ask if he still uses his special blanket. He says "No". I ask "Should I find it for you?" He nods and shows me where it will be. He snuggles down on the settee with his blanket, quilt and me and goes to sleep after listening to a story.

What seems to be an additional stressor for Harry at 3 years 1 month, is that Uncle Paul goes away to Germany for a month. Uncle Paul is high on Harry's hierarchy of preferred adults and has been caring for Harry some days each week. Soon after this, 'Harry was asleep in the car coming back from Ikea. When he woke up, he began looking out of *the window. He pointed at some calves, saying "They've lost their mummy and daddy. They're far, far away at Peter and Carla's house" '*. Peter and Carla live in Bournemouth and Harry has been to visit them there. This is 3 weeks after his daddy has been away to Bournemouth for the weekend. Is Harry again expressing his fear of losing his parents?

Harry is due to start nursery in September. His family worker, Lorna, visits him at home several weeks before he starts nursery. He tells me about Lorna visiting.

> *'Harry said Lorna did not have a Dad.*
> *I asked "What happened?"*
> *Georgia said "He died".*
> *Harry said "He died". Nodding his head.'*

At this time, Harry's main concern seems to be with everyone's dad. He is interested in Lorna's dad. Actually, Lorna's dad is not dead, so maybe Harry is speculating that Lorna's dad is dead because he does not know him?

Towards the end of Uncle Paul's 4 weeks away, Harry decides that *'We're going on holiday . . . to Germany . . . to see Uncle Paul'*. He seems to be trying to deal with his loss by planning (in his head) to join Uncle Paul in Germany. When Uncle Paul returns, they go swimming and *'Harry never leaves Paul's side'*. A few days later, however, *'He seemed a little unsure about Paul and about moving (looked serious and seemed to think deeply)'*.

A couple of days before the actual move, Harry (aged 3 years 2 months) is playing with the two teddies, Tim and Tom, at our house: *'Got Tim and Tom, undressed Tim – called him the dad, then the mum. He laid him on the floor and said he was bathing him. Cuddled Tom. Was a bit anxious when he noticed it was getting dark outside'*. Is Harry indicating what he needs (soothing and cuddling) through his play with the teddies?

How we help Harry to rise to the challenge of moving house, starting nursery and developing new routines

Moving house

Harry's parents carefully plan the move. They visit the new house several times while negotiating the mortgage. Colette talks to the children about what will happen in terms of each day and each week. On the day of moving, Harry and Georgia are fully involved in choosing which toys to take to their mum's house. They spend several hours loading Georgia's wooden trailer with toys and walking from dad's house to mum's, unloading the toys and then walking back. That evening their dad brings the children to our house for dinner. This may have been a conscious effort on his part, to show the children that they were not losing their mum or her family. They stay overnight with their dad at his house and only sleep at mum's house for the first time the next day.

Although the children have several months to get used to the idea of living in two houses, the reality still causes them pain. Harry is 3 years 2 months when his mum moves out. It seems as though he has to experience living in two homes for himself to understand what it means. Everything changes for the whole family. Smart *et al.* (2001) report: 'Co-parenting can be described as a series of mini-bereavements for some children' (p. 134).

Harry's parents make a conscious decision to live close to each other geographically. They decide to share the care of the children. This means that on five nights a week the children spend the evening and sleep overnight at their mum's home. On the other two days, they spend the day and sleep overnight at their dad's home. The arrangement means that they see both parents most days and that there are many brief separations each week. It could be argued that many brief separations cause more pain and distress for Harry. On the other hand, the pain of separation is for a short time each time and he may quickly build up trust that he will soon see the parent he is missing. It may be helpful to think about whether Harry has established a 'secure' or 'insecure' pattern of attachment (Holmes 1993; Bowlby 1998). If his attachment pattern is secure, then he has a basic belief or trust that his carers will be there for him and keep him safe. At reunion, he will be pleased to see each parent. If his pattern is insecure, then he will be anxious and, at reunion, will avoid contact, be angry, clingy or confused (Holmes 1993: 105). Harry is always pleased to see either parent and is able to tell each when he wants to see more of the other parent.

Bowlby (1998) says that 'Whether a child or adult is in a state of security, anxiety or distress is determined in large part by the accessibility and responsiveness of his principal attachment figure' (p. 43). It is difficult to say who Harry's principal attachment figure is. He is close to his mum *and* dad. The new arrangement means being with them one at a time. Smart *et al.* (2001) point out that in this situation 'being with one parent involves them in being apart from the other' (p. 69). In their interviews with children from split families, Smart *et al.* discovered that children do not necessarily experience this as losing something precious, as long as the arrangement is established and they can rely on it.

Being comforted

A couple of weeks after moving, when Harry is 3 years 3 months, the children stay at our house overnight. In the evening, they bathe their feet in lavender and water and have them massaged with cream: *'Harry particularly liked getting cream out of a pump-action container and rubbing it on his own legs, feet and hands'*.

Although he can be comforted, *'Harry woke up and cried first thing in the morning'*. Harry would stay overnight with us about once a month and it is unusual for him to cry. Does Harry suddenly remember, when he wakes, that life is different? That mummy and daddy have separated? Is he expressing his sadness about the split? That morning, he and Georgia spend about an hour in the bath playing with water and containers.

Expressing his feelings

Twice, during this visit to us, when the children are playing, Harry is desperate to have the bigger of two objects. What does his desperation signify? Does it signify his need for more comfort? Or his need to feel stronger and bigger and therefore to be entitled to the bigger object? Or is he seeing his sister as a rival and therefore pitting himself against her? Isaacs (1933) points out that 'hostility and aggression' can 'spring from feelings of inferiority' (p. 454). She notes that 'as helplessness grows less, so does hostility and aggression'. Does Harry feel helpless at this point? Is he showing his desire to have both of his parents?

Isaacs (1933) says that 'In the last resort, one's possessions are felt to be extensions of the self . . . What is mine becomes (in my feeling) a part of ME' (p. 225). So, wanting the bigger of two objects may be simply saying *"I am here. I am important. Consider me"*.

Helping Harry to cope with moving

A few weeks after moving, Harry becomes really distressed at his mum's house. He will not be comforted. The next day we buy the children a disposable camera each. We suggest that they each take photos of both houses and make books:

> 'Harry really enjoyed it. He took photos of the living-room, garden, his and Georgia's bedroom and the kitchen at Colette's house. Then we walked through the estate to Ian's. Mostly he wanted to go in the garden and took several photos – wanted to photograph each part of the garden. Then he took photos of the living-room and both bedrooms. Got on his bed and I took a photo of him and got on Ian's bed and again I took a photo. Did not want to photograph the kitchen'.

Harry displays a strong 'connecting schema' at this time (Athey 1990). It is difficult to work out what comes first – the connecting schema or the split, resulting in the desire to connect. When we look at the photos of Ian's garden taken by Harry, they give a comprehensive picture of the garden from one side to the other. You can literally line the photos up and gain a view of the whole garden. They connect with each other. Piaget (2001) stated that 'Affective life and cognitive life . . . are inseparable although distinct' (p. 6). Harry's affective life gives him the motivation to want to capture, on camera, the whole of his dad's garden. He applies his cognition to lining up and photographing each section in turn so that he captures the whole of the garden. The process of taking the photos gives Harry an opportunity to talk to his parents and grandparents about the two houses and what they mean to him.

Starting nursery

Harry (aged 3 years 4 months) starts nursery a few weeks after his parents separate. Ian reflects: "*He was familiar with all of it. We used to take him to drop-in from when he was a young baby. He used to go on the rocking-horse at drop-in – I would sit nearby*". The home visit from Lorna and 2 weeks settling-in time seem to help Harry to feel comfortable in the nursery. The nursery provides a predictable environment for Harry on four afternoons a week. He can be autonomous by choosing what to explore in the workshop environment. Lorna is in 'dialogue' with both of Harry's parents (Whalley 2001). She helps him to connect his experiences together.

Over time, Harry gets to know the other adults in the nursery. Several months later, he chooses to talk to some people about his complicated life. Harry (aged 3 years 10 months) tells Val that he did not want two fire engines for Christmas. Does he mean "*I do not want to live in two houses*"? He tells Angela that he has three houses, mum's, dad's and James's. (James is his best friend, who lives next door to dad. Harry and Georgia often stay at James's house.)

Harry has a strong connecting schema, which is supported at nursery by having string, magnets and construction toys (Athey 1990). Harry enjoys using the two pulleys in the covered, outside area. He seems to solve an equation by attaching one shoe to each pulley. He discovers that he can keep the shoes level and balanced by pulling the two strings simultaneously and with equal force. Might the equation mirror the situation in his family? Does Harry need to see and relate to his mum and dad equally to achieve a balance?

Generally, being at nursery appears to help Harry to connect his life and play together. He seems familiar enough with the environment and the people not to experience it as yet another change and threat to his security.

Getting used to new routines

Harry's life, over the few weeks before starting nursery, has changed irrevocably. Starting nursery is still an exciting adventure for Harry. He still has that ability to become 'deeply involved' in exploring objects in his environment (Laevers 1997). It is most helpful for Harry's family worker to know as much as possible about his pattern of care and the people he spends time with. With this detailed knowledge, Lorna talks to Harry about the people who are important to him and about the places he goes with them. She reassures him and clarifies who is picking him up each day. She also provides exciting, challenging things for Harry to do at nursery. He gets used to the new routine by being reassured, comforted and challenged by what he does at nursery.

Facing a fresh challenge

Five months after moving, when Harry is 3 years 7 months, the children face a fresh challenge when their mum takes them abroad on holiday for a week. She recalls: *"Both children cried every night for Ian"* but that *"the crying was started by Georgia"*. Colette feels that *"Georgia's existence is more led by people than his"* – Georgia is more of a people person, whereas Harry can become totally absorbed in what he is doing without needing people as much. When they cried for their daddy, their mum would talk it through with them. They had a book of photos of their important people with them. They would ring their dad every day. She feels that it was OK for them to be upset. Holmes (1993) notes: 'The way a parent handles a child's response to separation is a key factor here – whether by accepting and encouraging the expression of feelings of anger and sadness, or by sweeping them under the carpet' (p. 162).

Georgia and Harry have been on several holidays with either mum or dad and Harry has developed his own ways of dealing with the separation. His mum recalls:

> *"What he used to do at first, was somehow cope with the separation, then at reunion spend a lot more time lying on me, cuddling me and spending time with me. Now he seems to anticipate the separation by lying on me, cuddling me, etc., prior to the separation".*

His dad says: *"If the children have been away with Colette, then he's desperate to come to my house as soon as they get back"*. Might Harry be making sure that he has equal access to mum and dad?

Strategies Harry develops for dealing with change and transitions

As the months go by, Harry gets used to living in two homes. During his year at nursery, he displays two new strategies, which may help him to express his feelings about change and transitions.

Wearing his hood up

From Christmas to about the end of May (from the age of 3 years 7 months to 4 years), Harry likes to wear a hooded top and frequently keeps the hood up. Wearing the hood up may be tantamount to saying, *"I can't hear you and I don't want to listen to you"*. Uncle Paul says that *"Harry wore his hood up for several months – maybe longer"*. Does having his hood up stop him from hearing and seeing? His dad says, *"The chances are he got his first hooded top for Christmas – I'm not sure whether he chose it"*. Harry seems to like wearing a hooded top and it seems to put him in control of whom he responds to. Uncle Paul says, *"I pulled it down a few times jokingly but he didn't like that, so I just let him have it up. He wouldn't go anywhere without it"*. Might it be a kind of communication? "I have had enough"? "I want to decide who to speak to"?

Being a dog

Towards the end of his nursery year, Harry (aged 4 years) becomes friendly with Adam, who is a few months older than Harry. They engage in role playing '101 Dalmations'. Harry enjoys being Lucky, the dog. Harry's mum says that whenever she broaches anything he does not want to talk about – for example, 'starting school' – he becomes Lucky, the dog. Lucky just barks and does not understand 'people talk' and, therefore, does not respond. Becoming Lucky seems to be a strategy that Harry uses for responding in his own time.

Making choices

When it comes to visiting school, what helps Harry (aged 4 years 2 months) is choosing who he goes with. He chooses to make an extra visit with Marcus and his dad. Harry's parents feel it is important for Harry to have an extra visit, as he is the only child from his nursery starting this particular school. However, a long settling-in does not seem to be equally valued by the school. His reception teacher wants to know *"What is wrong with Harry that he needs an extra visit?"* The school policy is 45 minutes for each child on transfer day. She observes that *"he seems quite confident"*. Harry's parents and nursery workers feel that it is important to familiarize him with the environment, people and routines. If Harry is to feel safe and secure at school and able to be involved, he needs to know who he will be with and what will happen (Bowlby 1998).

Shortly after starting school, Harry's conversations at home are about which children in his class have the same names as children he knows at nursery. Again, he seems to be trying to make connections between his current knowledge and the new context of school.

Summary

In this chapter, we have been considering:

- how Harry, despite his language delay, communicates his needs;
- how Harry develops his interest in other people and uses stories and role play to learn about relationships;
- the ways in which Harry expresses his feelings about his parents' separation;
- how we help Harry to understand and cope with changes in his life;
- how Harry develops his own strategies for remaining in control of what happens in his life.

Table 4.1   Schemas mentioned in Chapter 4

Connection
Envelopment (hood up)

In the next chapter, we will consider how Harry learns to communicate, use language and become literate.

5 Harry learns to communicate, use language and become literate

We see in Chapter 4 how Harry communicates with other people through using sounds and gestures. His sister, Georgia, is often the interpreter of his meaning. She is his advocate and, with her help, he does not become too frustrated when the adults around him cannot understand his unclear speech forms.

Research has shown that the ability to develop language is innate (Pinker 1994; Gopnik *et al.* 1999). Many researchers believe that other people play a major role in helping young children to develop language. McDonagh and McDonagh (1999: 4–5) state:

> By examining interactions between children and their mothers (or other 'caretakers') researchers have established the existence of 'motherese', speech that is produced by an adult (or older child) in interaction with a child whose linguistic competence and cognitive development are perceived as limited.

Gopnik *et al.* (1999) note that 'Recent studies show that the well-formed elongated consonants and vowels of motherese are particularly clear examples of speech sounds . . . make it easier for infants to map the sounds we use in our language' (p. 130). Pinker (1994: 40) attributes less of the learning to motherese, as he points out that in some cultures, 'they do not speak to their prelinguistic children at all, except for occasional demands and rebukes' and yet the children still develop fully grammatical language. Trevarthen (2001) says that 'The word meaning is not important' but that 'When an affectionate parent talks to a baby, a rich musical quality comes into the voice.

Motherese has a special clear rhythm and melody, as well as transparent emotional qualities of pitch and timbre'. These interactions are a kind of emotional synchronizing of mood and shared interest. The main thing, according to Trevarthen, is 'that an infant's companions encourage a partnership of interest'. In other words, communication with Harry is enhanced if we interact using our shared interests as the focus.

This chapter is divided into sections:

- Harry learns to communicate and to use symbols
- Learning to write
- Learning to read

Harry learns to communicate and to use symbols

Just as we attribute meaning to Harry's early actions and sounds, he learns to use gestures and sounds to communicate with us.

Harry uses actions and words to express his feelings

When Harry is 1 year 3 months, '*he expresses his anger by throwing a candle when I ask him not to put it in his mouth*'. A month later, '*Harry says "Ma?", then throws his biscuit when he realizes we are going to the park without his mum*'. (Although we have explained and he has waved "Bye" to his mum, the reality is still a shock.) We can help Harry to come to terms with how he is feeling by interpreting his actions and naming what he might be feeling, for example, saying to him "You seem to be feeling cross because mummy is at home and not here with us".

At 3 years 4 months, Harry is able to articulate his own feelings: '*Harry and Georgia are staying overnight at our house. As Colette left, Harry began crying. He said "Me feeling sad cos mummy gone to my new house". I said that it was OK to feel sad and that I feel sad sometimes*'. Laevers (1997) would say that Harry's 'well-being' is high because he is 'in touch with his feelings'. Harry may be expressing his deep sadness about the new house as well as his sadness at this short separation.

At 5 years 1 month, Harry draws a picture and tells us a story about '*a sad worm*'. '*He's a sad worm cos he hasn't got any mouth or nose . . . and he's asking people to be his friend and they are saying "No"*'. Harry is communicating his ideas about why the worm might feel sad.

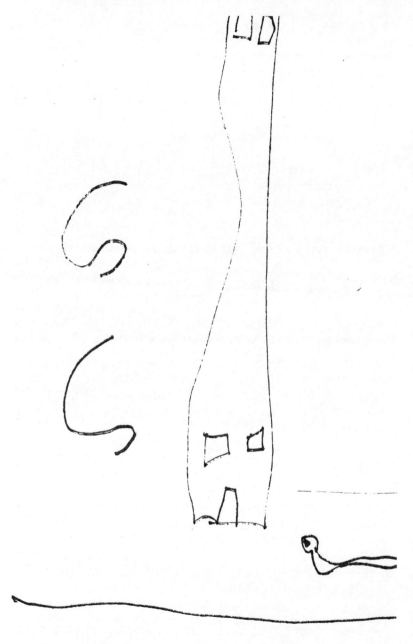

Figure 5.1 A 'sad worm'.

Harry develops his ideas about 'all gone'

Harry uses the phrase 'All gone' with gestures to convey a range of meanings. Bancroft (1995: 64) refers to a study of six children by Leslie Rescorla (1980) of the 'over-extensions' that young children use in their first 75 words. She found that 'in about 25 per cent of the cases', children were indicating something 'abstract' like the 'absence' of something. The example given in her study is the use of the word 'doll' to indicate that the doll is not in the crib. In a similar way, Harry seems to over-extend the use of 'All gone'.

When Harry is 1 year 7 months:

> *'Harry loves Christmas trees. Colette showed him ours out the back and not yet decorated. He kept going and touching it, coming to fetch us and gesticulating "All gone". (We assumed he meant "No decorations on the tree"). I told him Pop would be decorating it later – he seemed to understand'*. He also gestures *'All gone'* towards the barbecue. We assume he means *'There's no fire'*. He seems to be noticing any change or transformation in appearance. At 1 year 7 months: *'Harry was not wearing a nappy, lifted his vest and touched his willy, then covered it up and indicated "All gone" '*.

Vygotsky (1986) tells us that it is 'word meaning' that is significant and that 'Each word is already a generalization' (p. 6). Vygotsky's view is that Harry is thinking and communicating his thoughts to us by his use of the phrase 'All gone'. Harry perceives something different in the environment and externalizes his idea and question to us by saying 'All gone'. He can use different intonations and gestures to convey slightly different meanings.

These observations Harry makes may be contributing to his knowledge of the 'permanence of the object' (Athey 1990: 38). Athey relates these explorations to the first year of life and also to versions of 'hide-and-seek' that evolve from those early explorations. Harry continues to play with the idea that an object may still exist even if it is hidden.

Harry explores ideas about 'lost and found'

Games are important to Harry. With an older sister and a group of older children in the close, games are part of his social context. At

1 year 10 months, Harry plays hide-and-seek with Georgia: *'They always hide in the same place (at the end of Georgia's bed). Georgia tells Harry to count. He says "More, more, more, more"* '. To play hide-and-seek, Harry needs some understanding of the rules of the game and the sequence of actions that make up the game.

At 1 year 11 months, Harry's favourite bedtime book is *Where's Wally?*, a book in which he has to find Wally among complex illustrations. Wally is not easy to find but Harry discovers over and over again that Wally is always somewhere on each page. At 2 years of age, Harry enjoys 'Where's My Teddy?,' a rhyming story about a teddy that is lost and finally found in the woods. Harry discovers the predictability of the story, during which, Eddy, the Teddy, is always found. At 2 years 1 month: *'Harry's eyes twinkle when I change some words in a song he knows well'*. He notices the change and is stimulated by it. Harry knows the song so well that small changes excite him and keep him interested.

At 2 years 11 months, Harry initiates a game that involves covering or hiding an object: *'Harry liked wrapping pieces of duplo in wrapping paper, bringing the "present" to Colette and singing "Happy Birthday to You"* '. Here we can see that Harry is using his own experience of birthdays to play out a scenario. This links with Nelson's work on 'scripts'. Engel (1995) describes Nelson's work: '. . . she emphasises . . . the role of language as a form of mediation that creates order in the world' (p. 33). Young children act out and tell themselves stories about frequently experienced events in order to understand. Engel (1995) says, 'By reconstructing experiences in a narrative form, children put events into a coherent, meaningful order, a sequence' (p. 34). This observation is made 2 weeks before Harry's birthday.

At 3 years 3 months, Harry is surprised when he goes to bed at his Grandparents house: *'Harry wanted to know "Where are all the people?" He meant the cuddly toys that were usually on the bed. I sent Georgia downstairs to fetch the teddies, Tom and Tim'*. Does Harry use *'the people'* as players in his made up stories?

At 3 years 6 months, the wrapping game becomes a guessing game:

> *'Harry had Colette's scarf – played "making a bed on the floor", "wrapping presents (a book with a scarf)", "wrapping" or "concealing" his hand. This became a guessing game which he repeated several times. He would wrap one of his hands in the*

scarf and ask "Where's my hand?" I would make several guesses,
e.g. "Is it behind the couch?" "Is it at nursery?" Each time Harry
would say "No" but seemed excited and would anticipate my next
guess'.

Aspects of this which seem important to Harry are the sequence of
events (it would not work if it was in a different order), the rules of the
game (it would not work without the cooperation of both of us) and
the excitement and anticipation (coming up with new ideas about
where his hand might be). A story, like this game, has inherent rules
that make it work as a form of communication.

When Harry is 3 years 7 months, he becomes interested in the
functional aspects of the 'presents' in a birthday game:

> *'Harry started playing my birthday – brought me two corks in a*
> *bag. Said "If you get some wine what's got no lids, you can put*
> *those two on them". I began reading what was on each cork and*
> *saying where it had come from. After a while, Harry said "Read*
> *the letters on there". He sang "Happy Birthday" each time he*
> *brought me my present. The third or fourth time he sang "Happy*
> *Birthday to Mop, Happy Birthday to Mop, and a Happy New*
> *Year!"*

This happens a week after New Year and 2 weeks before Georgia's
birthday.

At 4 years 11 months, Harry plays a wrapping game. This time he
wraps something different each time:

> *'After a long time, Harry used wrapping paper and sellotape – kept*
> *finding different things to wrap and, after carefully wrapping with*
> *lots of sellotape, would take it to Georgia to open. Sometimes she*
> *would guess what was inside – he didn't mind. He never wrapped*
> *the same thing twice'.*

This occurs 3 weeks before Harry's birthday. Is he anticipating what
might happen on his birthday? Three days later:

> *'Harry initiated a game of "I spy" – he knows how to play – is*
> *using the correct beginning letter. He wanted me to "give in". Kept*
> *saying "Do you give in?" Played hide-and-seek – liked counting (to*

50) and shouting "Coming – ready or not". Hid under our quilt twice. Georgia says he usually uses her last hiding place each time'.

Three days later, Georgia plays *'Charades'* and Harry does the timing. At 5 years, *'Harry taught me how to play "Black Jack". He could keep 4 or 5 instructions in his head at a time. He beat me twice. Played "Snap" but laid his cards on the floor so that he could win'.*

So what is Harry learning from playing these games? He seems to pursue certain themes and to involve other people by asking them to guess. Birthdays appear to be a catalyst for practising and revealing his knowledge of the birthday 'script'. He uses his whole body (as in hide-and-seek), various objects as symbols (to represent presents) and cultural tools (like playing cards and letters of the alphabet).

Piaget and Vygotsky would agree that 'games with rules' are the highest form of play (Bruce 1991: 36). They would see Harry developing and learning and, eventually understanding complex shared rules. Bruce, however, sees creativity as of equal importance and, therefore, says 'we need both . . . games and free-flow play' (p. 105). She goes on to say, 'Games can fulfil all the features of free-flow play, except that they have rules which lead to certain specific outcomes'. When human beings 'are driven towards free-flow play' they know 'how to ignore or break pre-set rules'. Part of learning rules is interpreting them in the light of current knowledge and concerns. We certainly see Harry create his own games and rules. He does, however, seem to move towards understanding the games and rules of his culture and these are an important form of communication. Understanding how to communicate using symbols can help Harry be creative at a higher level.

When Harry covers or conceals objects or himself, Athey (1990) would say that his interest may be the concept of 'inside'. He explores these ideas at a *motor level* when he covers his willy with his vest. He learns that his penis is 'inside' a cover and cannot be seen (because he cannot see it).

Harry explores ideas about 'inside' at a *symbolic level* when he wraps up an object and uses it to represent a birthday present. He practises the whole scenario of 'wrapping – offering – singing – watching the opening of the present and subsequent surprise' many times.

Harry is using the idea of 'inside' at *thought level* when he plays 'I spy' and holds the answer 'inside' his head while we guess. He cannot hold it inside his head for very long and wants us to *'give in'*. He demonstrates that he can hold a set of rules 'inside' his head when he teaches me to play Black Jack.

Learning to write

Like many boys, Harry's route into learning to write is later than most girls and links with his earlier interest in action, construction and role play (Pahl 1999). He is less inclined than his sister to make marks on paper at an early age. We see in Chapter 3 that Harry gains the necessary physical skills needed for writing through playing with tools, string and construction materials.

The marks Harry makes

Learning to write is not simply learning to copy symbols. Kress (1995) tells us that 'the drawing of a line is an intensely physical, bodily activity, just as much as it is an intellectual cognitive one' (p. 15). He calls learning to write 'an act of constant transformation' (p. 18) of understanding and reconstruction. He says, 'Writing is the embodiment, the coding into muscular memory of meaningful action' (p. 15).

The records show that when Harry is 2 years 4 months, he begins drawing *'circular marks'* on paper. At 2 years 10 months, *'Harry paints up/down lines on paper'*. When he is 3, he is playing with 'Tap-it' (hammer, tacks and small wooden shapes on a board). He makes *'H for Harry twice on the board'*. Three weeks later, Harry notices that when he lays golf clubs on the ground, the cross shape is like *'someone's name'* (see Chapter 7 for the full observation). It looks a bit like 'H' for Harry. At 3 years 1 month, Harry begins to draw intersections or crosses. He draws a grid and calls it *'a crocodile'*. At 3 years 2 months, Harry is sensitive to 'grid-like' shapes in his environment: *'Harry kicks the ball skilfully into a net in the garden. Colette says he has been using rackets in all sorts of ways – bats, skis, swords, etc.'*. At 3 years 4 months, Harry draws *'kisses and cuddles for mummy'*.

For the next few months, most of Harry's drawing and writing is done on the computer both at nursery and at our house. When Harry is 3 years 11 months:

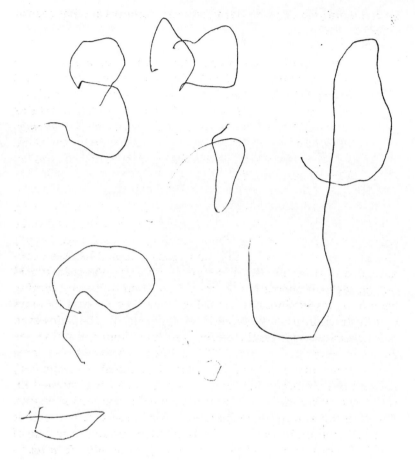

Figure 5.2 'Kisses and cuddles for mummy'.

'Harry's determination and persistence are obvious on the computer – he is wallowing in the Rover game now but Georgia asked for Word. Both children typed like a "typist" both hands/ all fingers approach. Georgia had typed something fast and said to Harry "What does it say?" He said "You're horrible and I love you", then laughed and said "You're horrible and me not love you!". Harry was much more prepared to take risks even on "Word" '.

Several months later, when Harry is 4 years 7 months and has been at school for a term:

> *'Georgia drew Teletubbies. Harry wanted me to draw for him – I did – he added parts, e.g. hands, TV around them. When we had drawn Po, I said "Why don't you write Po – it is just 'P' and 'o'." He checked out with Georgia – "Is Po just P . . . and Orange Oscar? No more letters?" Then he wrote it. He was very aware of his mistakes/poor form when drawing – used a rubber and scrapped one version of Lala when he had added layers to the ears and was not happy with the result'.*

Sadly, Harry seems to lose confidence in his own ability for a while after starting school. The goals seem to have shifted and to be about 'performance' rather than 'learning' (Dweck and Leggett 1988). Up until now everything Harry has attempted has been connected to his own interest and exploratory drive. Vygotsky would see Harry's spontaneous development in relation to literacy, lagging behind the instructions that are being offered. Vygotsky (1986) says that 'instruction usually precedes development' (p. 184). However, 'it is necessary to possess the means of stepping from something one knows to something new' (p. 187). If Harry is being offered some new learning that is within his 'zone of proximal development', then he can connect what he already knows and is interested in, with the new knowledge. Harry needs a means to use his strengths. Harry continues using the computer at our house and, when he is 4 years 9 months, he produces sheets of letters and numbers, one of which he gives to me and his mum, saying: *"I've cutted it in half – that's fair"*.

He also practises writing names on the computer. The computer helps to restore Harry's confidence while he is learning to crack the alphabet code. What motivates Harry to write seems to be lists and family names. When he is 5 years 1 month, he is interested in upper- and lower-case letters and in dividing the paper.

It helps if Harry has a genuine reason to write. In July, when Harry is 5 years 2 months, we are preparing for a family party. Harry makes a list of the boys coming to the party. Harry seems to be motivated to do this because of his continuing interest in gender and identity (see Chapter 1). Harry's drawings become more complex. He often incorporates writing into his drawings. When he is 5 years

jhfftri766668tutigffjh
figjjujgtiugtiotgujitui
tijit,jugt86yit86uyit8

658795oui659tiur86
576754m,jgiuig
eeee

Figure 5.3 'I've cutted it in half'.

pop
po
georgia tait
harry tait

georgia

Figure 5.4 Harry practises writing names.

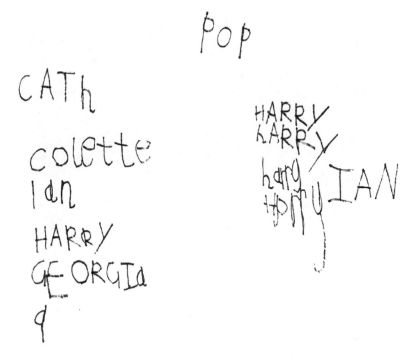

Figure 5.5 Harry is interested in upper- and lower-case letters.

7 months, Harry makes a list of Christmas presents and also a list of what he wants for his next birthday.

Occasionally, Harry is motivated to make and write little books at home. An example is one made and written when he is 5 years 7 months. He focuses on actions:

- the people clapping
- the man playing
- the man just going to play

And the functions:

- the piano has an OFF/ON button

This piece of writing and drawing is important in both charting

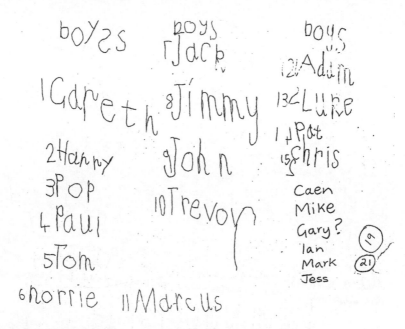

Figure 5.6 Harry's list of the boys coming to the party.

Harry's development and in valuing the interests and concerns that Harry brings to his writing.

Learning to read

Although our impression is that stories are not Harry's main interest, he listens over and over again to stories both at home and at nursery. Quite a few of Harry's favourite stories have been mentioned in this book already.

Harry's motivation for listening to stories

Harry's sister, Georgia, loves listening to stories from when she is very young (Arnold 1999). Therefore, even as a baby, Harry hears stories being told to Georgia and may view story telling as enjoyable times spent with adults. There is no pressure for him to listen but the opportunity is there if he wants to take it up. At 1 year

Figure 5.7 Harry incorporates writing into his drawings.

3 months: '*I was telling Georgia a story "Zoo" in which there is a little boy called Harry. Harry came over and listened*'. We become aware that hearing the name Harry mentioned sparks off Harry's interest in the story. So, subsequently, we look out for stories about different

Play station., station., woch., tom and jerry cake., cuddal toys.,

Christmas
lisd

New Bike. 2 New Nintedno Games. action man. New cuddly toys. New woch. New Games. New camera. New pichas. New picha fame.

Figure 5.8 A Christmas list and birthday list.

Harrys. This helps Harry to recognize his name and also to identify with all sorts of adventures and emotions experienced by other Harrys. Recently Harry (aged 9 years) said to me about this book, *"If you make the book a bit more exciting, like Harry Potter, you might sell more copies!"*

We help Harry to make other connections between the stories we tell and his world. One example is Alfie in the Shirley Hughes series of stories. Alfie has a comfort blanket like Harry does, so we draw his attention to that.

Being able to follow his interests in stories also motivates Harry. The records show that, although the children never have a household pet and Harry is fearful of dogs at times, he is interested in animals from a young age. Taking the children to the park or zoo where they can have some first-hand experience of seeing animals fosters this interest. These trips often spark off Harry's interest in rhymes and stories. When Harry is 1 year 3 months, we go to the park and see the ducks: '*Harry is completely fascinated by the ducks – I sing "5 Little Ducks"*

to him and he listens': A few days later: 'he brought me the "Fluffy Duckling" book and pointed at the duck and at the dog'.

When Harry is 1 year 5 months, we go to the zoo: 'Harry specially
liked the lions – he stood at the barrier and roared'. The journey was over
an hour and on the way home in the car: 'Harry enjoyed stories "Little
Fluffy Duckling" several times, "Hungry Caterpillar" and one about a
farm'. A few days later: 'As soon as I sat down, Harry came over with his
Baby Animal Book. He was indicating the elephant and making trunk
movements with his arm. Then he made a monkey face. He was making
more differentiated sounds too'.

On another trip to the zoo, when Harry is 2 years: 'Harry mostly
liked the giraffes. He is saying lots of new words including "giraffe" '. When
Harry is 3 years 11 months, we go to London Zoo on the train. This
time 'Harry liked the crocodiles, lion cubs, penguins, bouncy castle, tunnels
when we were travelling. He said the underground map was a long one'.

We notice Harry differentiating between written symbols

When Harry is just 2 years old, he can tell the difference between his
two identical toy double-decker buses. One says number 10 on the
front and the other says 15. At 2 years 9 months, Harry plays with the
Scrabble letters: 'He placed the letters on the ledge all the right way up
(chance or design we wonder?). He identified H, G and then A for Abbie
(Abbie was visiting us)'. At 2 years 11 months, Harry follows Georgia's
lead and plays 'Heads or Tails?' with a pound coin. This play seems to
link with a further development in Harry's thinking. We notice that
Harry can consider alternatives and begins to understand past and
future.

Harry's thinking becomes more flexible

When Harry is 2 years 7 months, we go to the station to see Eloise off
to Liverpool:

> 'Harry was very interested in the trains, track, where they were
> coming from and going to (directions). He noticed the wheels on
> the trains. At home we had lunch and Harry ran his bread along
> the table saying "It's a train". He bit some off and then said "It's a
> car". Told Ian one train was going to London and indicated "this
> way" and "that way".

Figure 5.9 Harry makes a book and writes a story in it.

The people are
clapping for the man

The man is lust
going to play the
Piano.

At 2 years 8 months, Harry is attending a meeting at the Centre with Ian: *'Harry is standing at the window watching the taxis go past. He has a very strong interest in directions "oos way" (pointing) and "oos way" (opposite direction)'*. When Harry is 2 years 10 months, Colette overhears Georgia and Harry categorizing the songs they both know into *'boys' songs'* or *'girls' songs'*. He also uses the word *'both'*. At 2 years 11 months, *'Harry refers to "yesterday" several times. Also "tomorrow". Says it's going to be his birthday and he's going to be 3'*. Two weeks later, when Harry is 3 years old: *'Colette says Harry has started saying "Might be – might be not", exactly what Georgia used to say at that age!'*

It appears that Harry is developing some flexibility in his thinking at this time. He can look back and forward in time, can *think* about putting objects in two separate groups and also consider two alternative options. Piaget (1959b) says, 'At about 3 . . . the imagined is something distinct from the real . . . this is the age when we meet with such words as "perhaps" ' (p. 231). Miller (1995: 29) describes the characteristics of Piaget's 'preoperational thought':

> Piaget characterizes preoperational thought as frozen . . . We also find a rigidity or lack of flexibility, of thought in the tendency to *focus on states* rather than on the transformation linking states . . . Perhaps the clearest example of the rigidity of thought is its *lack of reversibility*. The preoperational child cannot mentally reverse a series of events.

Maybe, through his interest in directions, tracks and moving vehicles, Harry has discovered a kind of metaphor for understanding time passing. It is impossible to see time passing but, on a track, he can see where the train has come from and is going to. He can also see trains running in opposite directions simultaneously. This may help with understanding alternatives.

When Harry starts nursery, he has a more fixed idea about himself at nursery. He dashes in on his first day (aged 3 years 3 months) and *'Lorna says "Come and see where you can hang your coat or bag, Harry". There is a name label above his peg. Harry says "Not that says 3!" '* At that moment, he seems to expect to see his age rather than his name on display. Labels like name and age appear to be synonymous with identity for young children.

Harry practises reading

The records show that one of Harry's favourite stories, over a long period of time, is 'The Tiger Who Came to Tea'. At 1 year 11 months: *'Harry pointed to my knee, said "Knee" and sat and listened attentively to "The Tiger Who Came to Tea"'*. At 3 years 7 months:

> *'The other new thing that Harry did was choose "The Tiger Who Came to Tea" and then relate it to me almost word for word, using the illustrations for clues. He particularly liked the page with "milkman", "boy from the grocer's" and "daddy". He told me the story three times'.*

At this stage, Harry knows his favourite story almost off by heart. Two weeks later, *'In bed he "read" the "Tiger Who Came to Tea" several times – again repeated pages 2 and 3 several times. In the morning he said "This is my bestest bit"'*.

At the age of 3 years 8 months: *'Harry is playing with the teddies, Tom and Tim. Said he was going to tell them "Goldilocks and the Three Bears". I got the "Tiger Who Came to Tea" book down and he told them that more or less word for word'*.

Much later, when Harry is 5 years 4 months:

> *'Harry chose "The Tiger Who Came to Tea". He said he would read it to me. He read about half of it, sometimes sounding words or making good guesses but mostly reading well and fluently. After he had read about half, he said he was tired and asked me to finish reading the story'.*

At this stage, Harry has been at school for about a year and has learned how to decode the words using his knowledge of the sounds. His spontaneous reading is beginning to connect with the instructions he is being offered at school (Vygotsky 1986).

Telling stories without written words

An idea that intrigues Harry is telling a story orally. He thinks about this and asks questions about it. He seems to understand when he is 3 years 4 months:

'I said something about Harry enjoying Goldilocks.
Colette said to Harry, "Did you hear Goldilocks at nursery?"
He shook his head.
Colette: "Where did you hear it?"
Harry: "It's in Mop's head".
Colette: "What's in your head?"
Harry: "Baa, baa black sheep".
Colette suggested "And Twinkle?" Harry agreed'.

At 4 years 6 months, Harry seems to have gained some more knowledge about what happens inside our heads: *'Harry told me the whole story of Goldilocks twice in the car including the different voices. He says he has a new friend, who can make up songs "out of his head". At home, he told Pop the Goldilocks story'*. A week later, the story is sparked off by what Harry notices at nursery:

'Harry came to meet me at nursery and noticed three seriated spoons hung on the cupboard door. He took them down and gave me the biggest, Maureen (our cleaner at nursery) the medium and kept the smallest. He told Maureen the whole story of "Goldilocks and the Three Bears" using the different voices.'

At 4 year 8 months, Harry is wondering about silent reading:

'Harry: "Everybody reads in their heads, don't they?"
Mop: "Do you?"
Harry: "When I read adult books I do" '.

Harry's experience, so far, is that children's stories are read out loud and adult books are read silently. So, maybe he thinks that when he reads adult books, he will read silently.

Reading as a catalyst for new learning

Making connections with written language often helps Harry to communicate with us about the things he is curious about. It helps us to understand what he wants to know about or what he is learning. At 5 years 8 months, he notices and reads the sign outside the Centre that says 'Parking for Minibus Only'. We had discussed the sign many times before. I had explained to Harry that we now park the minibus at the 'Children's Home' across the road, as there are people there day and night to keep an eye on it. We had had the windows broken several times at night when it was parked outside the Centre. He has obviously been thinking about this:

> 'Harry asks, "At the house where the minibus is, do they have food?"
> Me: "Yes".
> Harry: "How can they go out and buy food if they are in the house all the time?"
> Me: "It's a children's home, so quite a few children live there and different people work there. One person might be there during the day, then someone arrives before they leave and stays all night".
> He looked worried.
> Me: "The children are quite big – 12 or 14".
> Harry: "Or a hundred?"
> Me: "I don't think they would be a hundred".'

Then Harry makes a fresh connection and takes the talk in a different direction.

> Harry: "We've got a new jigsaw in my class that's got 100 pieces".

Harry's awareness of words increases. A week later, aged 5 years 8 months, Harry notices 'POP' written by Georgia and says "You know 'POP'?" "You POP out (pulling his jumper outwards from his body to explain)". "It's the same word!" "Two words!" I say "Two meanings – same word". A few weeks later, Harry (aged 5 years 9 months) hears Pop say "Spaghetti Carbonara" and comments "He speaked a different language!"

Harry attends speech therapy during his first year at school and his speech becomes much clearer. He grows in confidence and can communicate some complex ideas orally. We go out for a surprise Indian meal for Pop's birthday when Harry is 5 years 10 months. Harry is very excited and keeps up the pretence that we are going out to take some rubbish to the tip until the very last moment:

> 'Harry was very talkative at the table – he related some good tales – jokes, things about school, Spanish and French words he knows. Several times he talked about W (Wicked Water Witch) looking like monster's teeth if you keep writing them (i.e. zig zags). He told

> *a complex story told to him at school about someone in Jesus' time*
> *escaping through a "narrow gap" across which a spider sub-*
> *sequently spun a web. The web made it look as though no-one had*
> *gone through.'*

Harry begins to enjoy reading anything that connects with his interests, for example, joke books, instructions for games, recipes when we are cooking, anything about Teletubbies or, subsequently, Pokemon. Mostly, he is interested in non-fiction. When Harry is 6 years 3 months the proofs for 'Georgia's Story' arrive. I am amazed to hear Georgia and Harry reading all of the bits of dialogue out aloud to each other. Harry likes to be 'Dad' or 'Paul' and they giggle very loudly at parts of the book.

Summary

In this chapter, we trace Harry's development of communication, language and literacy. We look at:

- Harry's communication through sounds and gestures;
- Harry using symbols to communicate ideas;
- the early marks that Harry makes and how these develop;
- Harry's struggle to connect his love of stories with learning to read;
- Harry as an articulate 5-year-old.

Table 5.1 Schemas mentioned in Chapter 5

Envelopment
Inside
Circularity
Up/down trajectory
Grid
Horizontal trajectory
Inside
Going through a boundary

In the next chapter, we will consider Harry developing mathematical ideas.

6 Harry develops mathematical concepts

Mathematics, like language and literacy, is generative. In other words, when Harry learns to use numbers, to understand concepts about shape, space and measuring, he is developing concepts that he can apply to new situations.

Piaget (2001: 163) tells us that thought is 'internalised action'. Harry initiates many actions that help him to understand his world and his particular culture. As we see in Chapter 3, Harry uses his whole body at first and then objects to begin to understand concepts. Just as he uses the stories told to him to understand his emotions, he uses the mathematical signs (like numbers), practices (like using the phone) and words (like 'on top', 'behind' and 'before') with which he is familiar to understand emergent mathematical ideas.

Pound (1999) says that 'children's mathematical development, like so many other aspects of their learning, strongly reflects the culture within which they grow up' (p. 2). Schiller (in Bruce *et al.* 1995: 132) tells of a little girl who could work out 'pretend shopping' accurately in her head because of her real-life experience. She does it over and over again correctly, but then 'I had glanced down at the completed sums on the small blackboard on her desk; in every case the answer was wrong'. What she is learning in school does not make human sense to her and is not connected to the learning that she does, spontaneously and from necessity, at home.

This chapter is divided into sections:

- Harry explores capacity, size and fit
- Learning to count
- Investigating length, measurement and equivalence

- Harry makes advances in his understanding of classification, positioning and rotation

Harry explores capacity, size and fit

We see in Chapter 1 that putting objects into containers and tipping them out fascinates Harry. We can discover what he is learning by continuing to watch and by providing different containers and materials to be contained. Harry's explorations help him to understand the properties of the various containers he uses. At times, he discovers that what looks like a container cannot contain what he is putting in it. When Harry is 1 year 8 months: *'Harry loved standing at the sink with the tap running – he used spoons, cups, etc. to fill with water and drink. Tried to fill a funnel'*. A funnel might have held something solid but not liquid.

Harry's interest in putting things into containers involves him in estimating capacity and in exploring size and fit. When he is 2 years 4 months:

> *'Colette described how he had spent a long time putting his cars into two lunchboxes and carrying them about a few days earlier. Harry heard and then indicated he wanted a lunchbox – Colette got one down for him – he immediately opened it and began putting cars into both sides. He rejected one truck that was a lot too big. He kept trying to close the box with cars in both sides. Georgia came in and said, "Put them all in one side and it'll close". He did and it did'.*

Here he rejects the truck that he estimates is too big to fit but fills both spaces and cannot close the box, probably because the cars slip towards the middle as he tries to close it. Georgia offers him a technique she has used and it works. Both the container and contents are inflexible.

At 3 years 1 month:

> *'Harry is playing in the garden with gravel and a small plastic ball with holes in it. He puts a piece of gravel through one of the holes – then says "It falls out". Colette explains that "it falls out because it is small" . . . then he begins putting handfuls of gravel through the gap between a post and the drainpipe' (video clip).*

Harry is becoming interested in matching the size of the object with the space it can go through.

When Harry plays wrapping games (see Chapter 5), again he has to estimate what he can wrap with a particular size of paper or material. When he is 3 years 4 months:

> *'Harry is playing with our big old telephone. He has large sheets of wrapping paper and is struggling to cover the phone completely. He tries using glue and sellotape to keep the paper together and around the phone. Finally, he gives up and wraps a cork'.*

Here Harry is struggling to wrap something quite big, which is an irregular shape and inflexible. He has enough paper but might need to join it together first to cover the phone completely.

At nursery, aged 3 years 6 months, *'Harry places small blocks inside large hollow blocks'*. The small blocks are a small version of the large hollow blocks. Both are inflexible but the shapes match. When Harry is 3 years 7 months, he is playing a Happy Birthday game when he describes the present he wants to give, in terms of his capacity to hold it. *'Me gonna get you another present – it's going to be really big, what me can hold'*.

At nursery at 3 years 10 months, *'Harry makes enclosures and places animals inside'*. His concern with placing objects inside enclosures is reflected in his painting. And Harry's estimations and explorations become increasingly refined. At 3 years 7 months:

> *'Harry and Georgia spend ages putting the mahjong tiles away. When they get to the last few, they realize they do not fit in the compartment. Georgia lifts the tray and compares the layout with the tray underneath. The tiles are not quite square and therefore need to be placed in a particular way to fit. They tip them out and begin again. Harry makes no comment but places each tile carefully one at a time until the job is finished and they fit them all in'.*

The involvement and persistence suggests that Harry gains some satisfaction from completing this.

Athey (1990: 197) points out that providing containers with 'a specific capacity' can help children to develop their ideas about volume and capacity. Although Georgia takes the lead in solving

Figure 6.1 Harry makes enclosures and places animals inside.

the problem in the mahjong example, Harry seems to understand and is involved in carrying out the related actions. This is a game that he uses again and again in different ways. At 4 years 4 months: *'Harry is using a pencil sharpener with a rotating handle. There were some fat pencils that would not fit. He had to select the pencils that would fit. At first he tried each one and then could estimate which would fit from looking at them'.* Again the sharpener and pencils are both inflexible.

Learning to count

Harry hears and sees numbers in his environment from a very young age. He learns to explore them before he gains a fuller understanding of their uses.

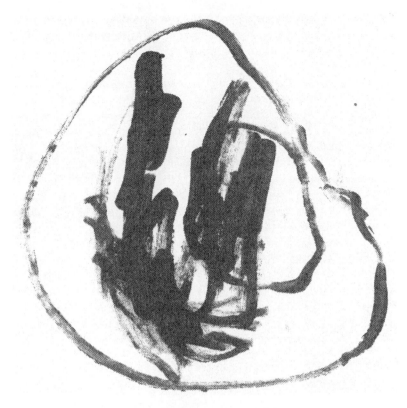

Figure 6.2 Harry paints an enclosure and paints inside it.

Harry explores quantities and numbers

The records show that Harry frequently carries objects around the house and outside as a toddler. He plays with pegs, money, corks, vehicles and a favourite plaything is a candle and holder. At 1 year 6 months:

> '*The other day, Harry played with 3 pieces of sponge for ages. He seemed to know that there were 3, that is he had dropped one without noticing it, but looked in his hand, saw 2 and began to look around for a third. Mostly he carried them around or put them into things*'.

Pound (1999) says that 'Babies of just a few days old . . . can recognize a group of up to three objects, showing surprise when objects are added or taken away from the group' (p. 3). Maybe we are slow to notice this ability in Harry.

Harry demonstrates his further understanding of particular amounts or quantities from when he is 2 years old: *'Harry asks for "2" when offered a biscuit'*. At 2 years 1 month, *'he seems to understand quantities of 1, 2 and 3'*. A week later, *'Talked about "more" and "two" and held up 2 fingers'*. At 2 years 2 months, Harry counts pairs of seats in a café by saying *"two, two, two, two"*. Harry has just become two and seems to be exploring 'two-ness' (Athey 1990: 180). A couple of months later (aged 2 years 4 months): *'We went to visit Georgia's school. When I went to the toilet Harry came with me and insisted on carrying 3 tractors. He struggled to carry them. Colette offered him a bag – he said "Bag" and happily carried them in a plastic bag'*.

We see in Chapter 5 that Harry enjoys listening to and telling 'Goldilocks and the Three Bears', a story that has a strong theme about 'three-ness' and 'one-to-one correspondence'. When Harry is 3 years 3 months, he has a new toothbrush that changes from red to orange under the hot tap and back again under cold water. *'I asked if it cost a lot. He said "Fifty thousand hundred" '*.

Learning to count

Young children can easily learn to count by rote, but Gelman and Gallistel (1978) suggest that there are five counting principles that children need to learn to fully understand how to count. The first is the 'one to one principle' (Maclellan 1997: 35). This means 'assigning a distinct counting word to each item'. There should also be 'a different counting word for each item'. We see in Chapter 5 that Harry (aged 1 year 10 months) counts by saying 'More, more, more, more'. At this stage, Harry understands about the rhythm of counting but does not use the actual number labels.

When Harry is 2 years 6 months, his mum hears him counting to 6 but he refuses to repeat it: *'A bit later Harry counts from 1 to 5 using his fingers in a one-to-one correspondence'*. When Harry starts nursery (aged 3 years 3 months), *'what he enjoyed most was counting things (everything in sight). He understands three-ness really well'*. A month later: *'We went to Kirby Hall and picked up conkers – Harry was really good at counting – got to six with no mistakes'*.

The second counting principle is the 'stable order principle', which means using the same number labels in the same order each time (Maclellan 1997: 36). It seems that Harry (aged 3 years 4 months) can do that up to 6. Harry practises representing numbers in different ways. When he is 3 years 8 months, Harry is at the workbench in nursery:

> *'he placed the nails precisely. He hammered 5 nails together in a group and said "Lorna that's number 5". I said "Yes and you have used 5 nails". Then "I'm doing another number 5" – he began to hammer more nails into the wood. His mum said he has been playing dice with Georgia all weekend'.*

This demonstrates the impact of home learning on Harry's play at nursery.

The third counting principle is 'the cardinal principle' – that is, that the last number represents the total number of items counted (Maclellan 1997: 36). At 2 years 4 months, when Harry is watching a Pingu video, *'he comments on "1 baby", "2 babies" and "3 babies". He holds up 5 fingers'.* At this stage Harry cannot quite connect the fingers he shows with the number of babies he discusses, but he is realizing that he has the means to represent quantity.

At 2 years 10 months, *'Harry counted "5 of us" correctly'.* Harry is beginning to understand the cardinal principle. At 3 years 7 months, Harry jumps ahead when he counts on and asks for *"3 more"* pieces of blu tack so that he has one for each corner of his picture. A month later: *'Harry counted up to 17 animals accurately'.* At 3 years 10 months, *'Harry counted up to 37 – there are 38 levels at which you can play Rover on the computer'.*

The fourth counting principle is 'the abstraction principle' – that is, that any items can be counted. Harry is using counting for different purposes and seems to be beginning to understand that any objects, whether seen or unseen, can be counted. When Harry is 5 years 8 months, and is interested in *'silent reading'*: *'Harry set up the wooden marble run so that some marbles would disappear (into a tunnel) – he began counting how many marbles went into the "magic" '.* He said *"We are playing Hide and Seek".* So now Harry is able to count and to hold in his head the number of marbles that cannot be seen.

The fifth counting principle is 'the order irrelevance principle' – that is, 'that the order in which items are counted is irrelevant'

(Maclellan 1997: 37). It is difficult to spot when Harry understands this. However, when aged 3 years 7 months, he and Georgia make up their own game with mahjong (see Chapter 7); he often counts the number of tiles and bones that correspond to his throw of the dice and then recounts them in a different order. He is checking that he has taken the correct number. This would seem to indicate his understanding of the order irrelevance principle.

Harry becomes interested in making comparisons

Early on, Harry frequently sorts toys, blocks and household objects in different ways. He often lines them up from smallest to largest. Athey (1990) says that 'Seriation and classification have their origins in early actions applied to a wide range of objects and, later, to events' (p. 41). When Harry is seriating objects according to size, he is noticing the similarities and differences between them. This physical sorting of objects helps Harry to understand numbers and related concepts.

When Harry is 4 years 10 months, we have a conversation about house numbers:

> 'Harry: "Your house is number 5".
> "My mummy's house is more than that".
> "My daddy's house is more than that".
> "That means you are littler than them" '.

Harry is trying to use logic by relating the two ideas of house number and physical size together.

At 5 years 5 months:

> 'Harry talked about Grandad looking older than a man at the Community Centre, who is 70; Grandad and Grandpop being about the same size; me being fatter than Nana (he said "She is very thin"). I said something about my living room being small. He said "Mummy's room is bigger than this" and "daddy's room is definitely bigger than yours" '.

Harry's estimations are realistic now. He seems able to spot an anomaly; that is, Grandad looking older than a man who is older than him. He even considers my feelings about being fatter than Nana.

At 6 years 5 months, we talk about another anomaly: '*In bed in the morning, we talked about birthweight and the anomaly that the firstborn usually weighs least. So although Harry's mummy is the eldest of our children, then Paul, then Eloise, his mummy was the smallest at birth, then Paul, then Eloise*'. Harry is interested and seems to understand.

Investigating length, measurement and equivalence

Harry explores length

We see in Chapter 1 that Harry enjoys 'carrying objects and placing them with people or in different locations' (transporting). Athey (1990) explains that 'When the youngest children toddled they simply *displaced* themselves. Later they picked up objects and *displaced* those' (p. 135). She goes on to say that 'When a two-year-old establishes *starting points* and *points of arrival* during *transporting* behaviour, he or she is presumed by Piaget to be experiencing physically early *equivalence* of *distance, length* and *speed*' (p. 136). Harry marks the distance he travels by leaving objects at his points of arrival. One aspect of the transporting schema is that he physically experiences the distance he travels. Another aspect is that he is gathering information about what the objects look like when distributed or collected.

Another early pattern or schema that Harry explores is 'making lines' (see Chapters 1 and 7). Nutbrown (1994: 62) tells us about a little boy called Adam:

> Adam fitted construction pieces end to end and placed them between the tables on the nursery floor to make a long line. In so doing, Adam was working on the concepts of length and space. He saw that he could add more pieces to increase length, and looking at his work he saw the length of what he had made in comparison with the floor.

In a similar way, Harry makes lines and surveys his work. At nursery, Harry often:

- extends the length of vehicles he rides by connecting trailers (e.g. aged 3 years 3 months);

- extends the train track by adding on pieces of track, bridges, etc. (e.g. aged 3 years 7 months);
- connects trains and carriages together to increase the length (e.g. aged 3 years 6 months);
- lines up trucks (e.g. aged 3 years 6 months);
- makes very long mobilo models (e.g. aged 3 years 7 months);
- uses the very long window pole to open windows (e.g. aged 3 years 9 months);
- listens to 'The Last Noo-Noo', a story that includes a long contraption for hooking dummies (e.g. aged 3 years 9 months);
- connects Lego after classifying it by colour (e.g. aged 4 years);
- carries a very long piece of guttering and uses it as a gun (e.g. aged 4 years).

Another way in which Harry explores length is by 'throwing objects'. At 1 year 8 months, Harry discovers that he can 'throw' or 'project' his voice all of the way downstairs from upstairs. *'Colette says that Harry stands at the top of the stairs and shouts "Dorda". Georgia goes to the bottom of the stairs and says "Yes?", but he doesn't know what to say then'*. A few days later, *'Harry spoke to me on the phone for the first time this evening. Colette said "Say Mop". He said "Mor" and then repeated it as though he meant/understood'*. Is Harry experimenting with projecting his voice and, therefore, intrigued by the phone?

Harry explores measuring

Harry's interest in length and distance continues. In his talk, he appears to be demonstrating a general sense of understanding where places are located in relation to each other. At 2 years 11 months: *'Harry talked about his house being "near" to my house'*. A few months later (aged 3 years 5 months): *'Harry recognizes that Marcus lives near to where Georgia goes to gymnastics'*.

Harry begins comparing the length of two similar objects. At 2 years 11 months: *'Harry argued with Paul over the length of the golf clubs. The bottom of the clubs was not level. He based his judgement only on where the top of the clubs reached'*. When Harry is 3 years 2 months: *'He had two paintbrushes and kept measuring them against each other'*. Two weeks later: *'Harry's concern was about standing the pens and lids on end'*. Might he be estimating the height of different pens?

Athey (1990) points out that 'linear measurement requires the co-ordination of three earlier schemas, a given *space* between two *end points*, the *connection* of standard units and *number*' (p. 190). At this stage, Harry is not using standard measurement or number but is comparing like with like. He needs the objects to be level at one end and may be achieving this by standing the pens on end on a level surface.

At 3 years 7 months, Harry is very amused and excited when he uses a 'blower' that extends when he blows it: '*A tissue accidentally gets caught up in the rolled up blower. When Harry blows it, the tissue flies out and floats to the floor. He tries putting a bran flake in it but the effect is not as great, that is, it drops quickly to the floor rather than floating down. Harry says "It's very funny!"* '. Here Harry is increasing the length by blowing and he can see the *rolled out* length as equivalent to the *rolled up* size.

Harry becomes interested in equivalence

Although Harry is interested in length and measurement over a long period of time, his burning interest is in the equivalence of wound-up string with unravelled string. He frequently studies what this looks like. At 3 years 3 months:

> '*Harry found parcel ribbon and unravelled it from the centre of the ball, asking Ian to hold one end while he stretched it across the room. He cut it and said it was like a skipping rope (held it at either end and tried to skip). Then he went upstairs with it and allowed it to trail to the bottom of the stairs*'.

As well as studying the equivalence between the wound-up and unravelled string, Harry has made a tool, the piece of string, to compare the length of the room with the height of the stairs.

At 3 years 8 months: '*Harry had a ball of string and told Colette it was really long – it would "go to Kettering" (5 miles) . . .*' (this conversation is referred to in Chapter 7). It may not be a coincidence that, on the same day, Harry thinks about and talks about 'time lines' that he cannot see: '*Harry asked about the sequence of family birthdays. Told me "My birthday's in May"* ' [future time] and '*asked for me when me a baby (on video)*' (the line of his past).

At 3 years 11 months, Harry explores equivalence of length in a very physical way when '*he walks around the post of the canopy*'

Figure 6.3 Harry walks around the post of the canopy.

winding string around as he walks. He is walking around in a circle, rotating the string around the post. At 4 years 2 months:

> 'Harry discovered string (which he had stashed in an old camera box) and looked really pleased. He wound it around 3 highlighter pens (together) and said they were "tied up". He asked for Pop's toy

cars down from a high cupboard and began to wind string around the transporter and cars. He laid the string on the floor, felt and looked at the length. Asked me to make "a hole" – he meant a loop'.

Here Harry may be interested in how a line becomes a circle and the equivalence between the line and the circle.

At 4 years 4 months: *'Harry and Georgia went to Wicksteed Park on Sunday. Ian said that Harry worked out, in his head, how he would spend the tickets he had on rides. (Some rides cost 2 tickets and some cost one ticket)'.* Now it seems that Harry can *think about* a number of tickets being equivalent to a number of rides when it is not only a one-to-one correspondence but a two-to-one correspondence. Harry seems to be internalizing ideas about equivalence.

Harry continues to be fascinated with string. When he is 5 years old:

'Harry came to nursery after school – got a ball of string. Made a small loop at one end and asked me to put a double knot in it. Then cut a long piece and made a bigger loop at the other end (again asked for a double knot to secure it). Trailed it along the corridor. It went from mid-corridor to the fish tank' (a distance of about 15 metres).

Later on the same day at our house:

'Looped one end of a piece of string around the leg of the coffee table. Looked around for somewhere high up to attach the string to. Tried connecting it to the metal plane on the mantelpiece. I explained that it would be dangerous if someone came along and knocked it down . . . Then he asked me to hold one end of the ball of string (I was in the dining room) while he walked upstairs with it. He told me it was by the phone upstairs. When Terry came in, he took him upstairs to see it. Terry said it was unravelled completely and placed on the bed near the phone'.

At this stage, Harry seems to be using a fixed starting point, that is, the leg of the coffee table or me holding the string. He seems to be interested in the string connecting points at different levels. He is also marking his journey upstairs with string.

These explorations into the oblique seem to connect with Harry's puzzle when he is 5 years 2 months:

> *'We went to town and parked at the top of the multi-storey car park. As we walked back from the bank, Harry pointed towards the gap leading to the Littlewoods car park. He said "That's very strange, you only need to go down a little bit there . . . but you have to go down a long way there" pointing towards the multi-storey'.*

This takes quite a lot of thinking about (even now). We are on level ground and can go down a slight slope into Littlewoods car park and then another slight slope on to the main road. Alternatively, we can step directly on to the top of the car park and then we have to drive down seven steep ramps as we go down to the ground and then on to the same main road. The two car parks exits are about 150 metres apart on the same road. At the time, I explained that the road is a hill and that the Littlewoods car park is nearer the top of the hill, whereas the multi-storey is nearer the bottom of the hill. This is true but does not completely account for the difference. I now think Harry poses a more complex problem of equivalence between the vertical route (steep ramps zig zagging up and down) and the oblique route (a longer, more gradual incline). This may contribute to his understanding of angles and triangles at a later stage. His sense of the triangle formed by coming down the multi-storey, going along the road and up the longer gentler incline to reach the same point is a 'spontaneous concept' (Vygotsky 1986), which connects with a related 'scientific concept' when he learns about right-angle triangles.

Harry makes advances in his understanding of classification, positioning and rotation

We see in Chapter 1 that Harry is able to identify 'males', 'babies', 'trees' and 'sources of light' as belonging together in groups. The urge to group or classify objects and people according to their similarities is a way that human beings learn about the world (Gopnik *et al.* 1999).

Children seem to come at this grouping of objects in two ways. First, using a word as a broad generalization of a class of objects – for example, 'dog' to represent all animals or 'dada' to represent men – before becoming more specific. Secondly, matching one object with another that looks similar. Harry does this matching when he is interested in twoness. At 2 years 1 month: *'Harry points at Colette's watch and then at mine'*.

Often Harry is thinking about gender issues when he is classifying things. When he is 2 years 10 months:

> *'Their routine at night currently involves singing songs before bed. Georgia was suggesting "Twinkle, Twinkle" and Harry was saying "No – that's a girls' song". In listening, Colette established that "Twinkle" and "Snowflake" are girls' songs and "Baa Baa Black Sheep" is a boys' song. When I asked about "Away in a Manger", Harry hesitated before deciding "It's a girls' song" '.*

When the family goes out to lunch for Paul's birthday and Harry is 3 years 4 months, *'Harry took Balou (one of the cuddly toys) and insisted on "boys on this side of the table" and "girls on that side" '*. Is he separating the genders so that he can identify and feel solidarity with the males?

Sometimes he reveals some of his underlying ideas about masculinity. At nursery, aged 3 years 8 months: *'Harry was hammering thick nails in and saying "These are the men" and then thin nails in saying "These are the women" '*. Is he linking strength and size with masculinity?

When 4 years 5 months: *'We went to Coventry. Harry was interested in which are "old" buildings – pointed at a church and said "That looks old" '*. At 4 years 6 months: *'Played Scrabble and Harry matched and named the letters'*. At the same age: *'Found four rabbit holes'*.

Harry is obviously *thinking about* groups of people doing similar things when (aged 5 years 2 months) he asks whether Pop and I play golf *"in a team"*?

When Harry (aged 6) becomes interested in Pokemon, this is the ultimate classification system for him to learn and he thoroughly enjoys the complexity of it. For a while, he carries his Pokemon Handbook around with him so that he can look things up as they crop up. Aged 9 years, he uses a large dictionary and atlas competently.

Harry explores positioning

Harry explores positioning by placing himself or objects in different positions, for example, on top of other objects. When Harry is 1 year

7 months: '*He tries to place a quoit on Georgia's head*'. A month later, '*he places a play person's tiny hat on his own head*'. We took this as evidence that he knows where hats are placed. We see in Chapter 5 that, at 2 years 9 months, '*Harry places the Scrabble letters the right way up*' and earlier in this Chapter that, at 3 years 2 months, '*he places pens and lids on end*'.

At nursery, aged 3 years 3 months, Harry likes to sit '*on top of the rocking horse*'. At 3 years 11 months, '*Harry uses the large barrel to go inside, through and on top*'. He seems to be experiencing the world from different viewpoints. At home Harry frequently plays with cars, play people and animals, placing them in different positions and looking closely at what he has done.

During these explorations of position, Harry seems to gain some new understanding about other people knowing where he is. At 3 years 7 months: '*Harry rang his daddy (on a pretend phone) and said "If he want me, me said ring me. Me told him where me are*" '. A month later at nursery, Harry says: "*Me tell you where me going so you know where me am*". His language changes over time too. At 4 years 8 months, Uncle Paul notes that '*Harry was talking about his Letterland Poster and began saying "It's at the top of . . . my bed", but changed it to "above . . . my bed*" '.

At 4 years 8 months, Harry is concerned when he gets a Teletubbies comic and Po (the smallest) looks bigger than the other Teletubbies. Colette explains that Po is nearer and, therefore, looks bigger. He seems to understand. When Harry draws, he experiments with placing objects in different positions. At 5 years 5 months, Harry draws a picture of fish in different positions.

Harry explores rotation

Understanding rotation and circularity are important aspects of mathematical development. Harry needs to experience the physical sensation of rotating his own body and objects in his environment to understand shape and angles (Pound 1999).

We rarely see rotation as the most obvious or most important aspect of Harry's explorations. On a trip to a Science Discovery Park, Harry (aged 1 year 10 months) '*seemed to like things that rotated: used a pendulum, sent ball bearings down a vortex, liked wheels, pulleys and vehicles*'. Through his explorations with play people and vehicles (see Chapter 3), Harry incidentally explores rotation. Sometimes this is

Figure 6.4 Harry places the fish in different positions.

partial, for example, when he moves the legs of the play people from a vertical to a horizontal position.

When Harry (aged 3 years 4 months) spends two hours connecting mobilo, his main concerns are *'connection'* and *'length'*. However, when he constructs a fire engine and places a ladder on top, *'He discovers that the ladder rotates and flicks it with his finger several times'*. Many of Harry's drawings are representations of circular or rotational movements.

Just after Christmas, when Harry is 3 years 7 months, *'he wanted the candles lit on the advent twirler. Twirled his body around and around while that was rotating . . . also used a kitchen timer to time his and Georgia's 5 minute turns with Pop's electric trainset'*. Several months later when Harry is 4 years 1 month:

> *'Suddenly seems to be rotating things – computer chair, globe (at nursery), pencil sharpener, pastry cutter. Asked me to look at the gate of the level crossing – he had opened it more than ninety degrees . . . Colette says that last night he wound a whole reel of cotton around the legs of the table and then wound it up again . . . also rolled up paper'.*

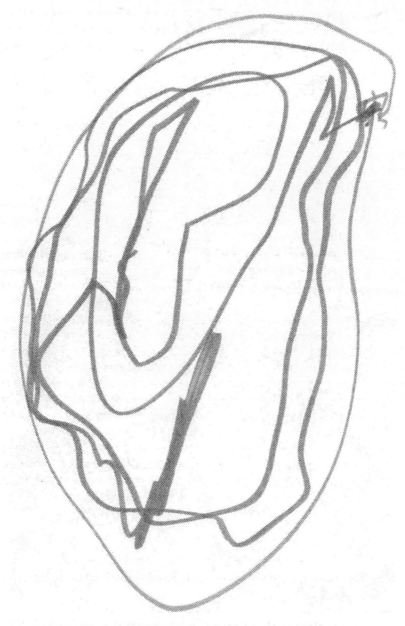

Figure 6.5 Many of Harry's drawings are representations of rotational movements.

The next day: *'Harry just rang me to tell me he's been doing loads of drawing and he's been going "round and round and round". Colette says he's been twirling his body . . . she's told him it's called rotation and he's aware of it'.*

On holiday (aged 4 years 3 months), Harry *'liked winding the swing around and then letting it go and watching it unwind'*. Athey points out that 'the energy released in "unwinding" is functionally dependent on the initial "winding up" . . . like a yo-yo or mechanical toy which produces linear movement energy' (personal communication).

What Harry is learning

Davies (1995: 92) says that children can absorb 'the circularity of movement' when they see others carrying out sequences of movements that they cannot yet perform. Harry's sister, Georgia, goes to gymnastics and he often goes and watches. Davies adds that children add to their 'personal movement repertoire' and then combine movements and practice. Harry has become aware of rotation and is practising rotating his own body and objects in his environment.

Circles, unlike lines, never really begin or end. They turn on an axis. Much later, when Harry is 5 years old, he is playing with butterfly clips and paper: *'He said "I could make a clock". He asked me to cut out a circle, then he cut out 3 hands (large, small and second). At first he was going to use one clip for each – suddenly he clicked that he only needed one clip for all 3 hands'.* This shows his understanding that the 'axis of rotation' on a clock is shared by the hands (Borowski and Borwein 1989).

Another aspect of exploring rotation is learning 'the vocabulary of rotation' (Nutbrown 1994: 60). Harry is using words like 'round and round' and Colette introduces the word 'rotation'. When he is cooking, he talks about 'stirring', 'spinning' and 'rolling'.

Summary

In this chapter, we have been looking at the mathematical concepts Harry develops by:

- exploring the properties of containers and what they contain;

- gradually gaining a sense of what counting means and learning to count;
- being interested in exploring equivalence;
- categorizing objects, songs and people;
- placing himself and objects in different positions;
- rotating himself, objects and drawing 'round and round' and by becoming aware of rotation.

Table 6.1   Schemas mentioned in Chapter 6

Containment
Going through a boundary
Enclosure
Size and fit
Threeness
Twoness
Transporting
One-to-one correspondence
Seriation
Trajectory
Rotation
Connection
Classification
On top

In the next chapter, we will be thinking about Harry's creative development.

7 Harry's creative development

To look at how Harry expresses his creativity, we must first establish what we mean by creativity. Often, in nurseries in England, we refer to 'the creative area', meaning the area where art materials are available for children to use. This is quite a narrow view of creativity. In fact, children are creative in all areas of the nursery. Certainly, the diary shows that Harry expresses his creativity through drawing, painting, model making, construction, small world play, imaginative and role play, having ideas, solving problems and making up games.

Csikszentmihalyi (1996) says that 'Creativity is a central source of meaning in our lives ... most of the things that are interesting, important, and *human* are the results of creativity' (p. 1). He goes on to say that creativity is what separates humans from animals. He finds creativity 'fascinating' because 'when we are involved in it, we feel that we are living more fully than during the rest of life' (p. 2). So, how do we recognize creativity in Harry's play and what helps him to be creative? We shall see that when Harry is 'deeply involved' (Laevers 1997), he is usually being creative. Fostering Harry's curiosity helps him to be creative. Csikszentmihalyi (1996) says: 'If too few opportunities for curiosity are available, if too many obstacles are placed in the way of risk and exploration, the motive to engage in creative behaviour is easily extinguished' (p. 11). Harry is encouraged to explore and to discover things for himself from an early age by being given a treasure basket containing a chain and heavy glass candleholders among other natural household materials. His parents trust that he will learn through manipulating these objects.

Vygotsky (1978) describes how everything that children learn begins in the 'interpersonal' world before becoming 'intrapersonal'.

During this process of 'internalization', several transformations take place. Vygotsky (1978: 56) uses the example of 'grasping', which becomes 'pointing' when people in a child's world attribute meaning to the primitive grasping. Gradually children learn to point and to mean "I want that" or "What's that?" We often recognize innovation in the way that young children 'externalize' their ideas. This seems to be creativity. When children are being creative, they are not simply imitating what they have seen or experienced, but are 'externalizing' an idea in a different form (Pahl 1999).

Tina Bruce (2001: 4) explains very clearly:

> The imagination makes images in the mind. Creativity is the process by which children turn these images into creations. They try out ideas, feelings and relationships in their role play or pretend play, make props for their play or find things to be used as play props. They might paint, make music, dance, make construction in block play, or make models with found materials or clay.
>
> In the context of play, creativity is more of a *process* than a product. The richer the creative process (the trying out of the imagination), the richer the product (the play scenario, the construction, the song, the dance etc.).

This chapter is divided into sections about:

- Making lines
- The importance of string
- Construction, role play and making models
- Bringing ideas forward from earlier first-hand experiences

Making lines

As we see in Chapter 1, Harry becomes very involved in making lines with small vehicles and animals at home. When he attends drop-in at the Family Centre, he finds more materials with which he makes lines, for example, maple blocks and a wide range of small world animals. His lines become more precise and he begins to group objects in particular ways, for example, largest object to smallest.

At 3 years 1 month, Harry is playing in the garden with a set of four metal golf clubs:

> 'Harry places the golf clubs on the ground end to end in a line. He stands back, looks down and smiles. Then he adjusts the end one before placing it perpendicular to the line. He moves the line across, making a "cross" shape with the two clubs. He places the next club near the cross, looks back and says "Aha". He places the two clubs across the line and says to his mum "That your name?" She replies "Not my name really – it's more like your name than anyone's I think". He shakes his head and says, "That not mine" '. (video clip)

Harry seems to recognize that the form he has created is like someone's name. He is right that it is not exactly like his own name, but he has a sense of its resemblance to something he has seen. Athey (1990: 94) points out that 'poor form is disliked'. Harry may recognize the similarity but reject the poor form of the grid shape.

When Harry is 3 years 7 months, he and Georgia are playing with a Mahjong set, which consists of small 'tiles' (cubes), 'bones' (narrow lines) and tiny di. They make up their own game and rules:

> 'Each throws the dice and picks up a corresponding number of tiles and bones. At first each make their own line by alternating a tile with a bone. After a while Harry joins his line to Georgia's. She goes off to the toilet and instructs Harry to take her turn. He manages to throw the dice for her, select the corresponding number of tiles and bones and add them to her end of the line, before taking his own turn'. (video clip)

Piaget (1962) and Garvey (1977) agree that games with rules are primarily social. Harry and Georgia negotiate a shared set of rules and stick to them to play their game together. The game depends on them being skilled enough to negotiate and follow a set of rules.

At 4 years 11 months, Harry is playing with the Mahjong set. He is very engaged for over an hour and appears to be making lines and other formations:

> 'Harry has placed the tiles in several rows. He makes a grid with bones and places a tile on top of it. I go closer and hear him

> *making crying and bleating noises. He explains that the rows of tiles are the "children and parents" and the grid is "the crib" with "Baby Jesus". Other tiles represent the animals, Mary and Joseph and the Kings. Harry is representing the Christmas Nativity Play at school including the audience.'*

Without close observation, we might think that Harry's play has not developed. Here he is using the tiles and bones as symbols to represent his earlier first-hand experience of the Christmas Nativity Play at school. Using the tiles and bones as symbols may be helping Harry to reflect on and understand what happened in ancient history and in his own recent history. Hobson (2002) explains that using symbols helps us to transmit an idea from one mind to another. As soon as I know that Harry is using the tiles and bones to represent people at the Nativity Play, I begin to understand his ideas about what is happening during the play. Hobson (2002) says that 'Symbols crystallize and then protect a child's ideas, so that the ideas can be thought with and thought about' (p. 274). They can also be communicated to another person.

The importance of string in Harry's play

Around the time that Harry starts attending nursery at 3 years 3 months, he begins using string. He explores using string in different ways and becomes 'deeply involved' in his play with string (Laevers 1997). The observational records show that, over a long period, Harry would use Teddy Tim's scarf (which is a flexible line) in different ways. When Harry is 2 years 8 months, he plays with Teddy Tim and Tom, a smaller Teddy: *'Harry played with Tim, kissing and cuddling him and Tom. He took Tim's trousers off, saying "He's not cold". He took Tim's scarf off. Colette tied Tom to Tim using the scarf like a baby sling – Harry seemed to like that. He looked pleased and called them "baby" and "daddy" '.*

Looking at this observation from a Vygotskian perspective, Colette carries out an action on the materials, which enables Harry to take the play further. Although she ties the teddies together, she does not tell Harry who she thinks they are. He expresses his own idea about whom the teddies are representing in his thinking. We saw in Chapters 1 and 4 that males are particularly important to Harry and his thinking here may be an indication that he wants to be connected to his Daddy.

Around the time of moving house, when Harry is 3 years 3 months, he plays with tape measures (again a flexible line). He is also interested in ladders (an inflexible line). At 3 years 4 months, Harry is at nursery: *'In the maple block area, Harry carried a long block calling it a "ladder" and trying out leaning it against things and reaching the "sky" with it'*. A few days later at our house, Harry uses pieces of mobilo (inflexible lines which can be joined together and bend at each join): *'Harry was very engaged with mobilo for a long time. He made a vehicle with a long extending ladder on top. When I commented "That's a really good ladder because it extends", he said "That's what ladders do" '*. It seems so obvious to Harry that I took that as evidence of his concern with the concept of 'reaching' and 'connecting'. Maybe Harry has seen an unfolding ladder.

Harry also shows an interest in playing with elastic bands (flexible enclosures). At 3 years 4 months, he goes to the Golf club with his Grandpop and plays with elastic bands *'for ages'*. A month later: *'Harry picked up lots of elastic bands . . . He spent a while putting them together. Then he hung some on the knobs of drawers. He tried to loop them around the leaves of a plant and placed some around a small cylindrical film case'*. When he is using the bands, his main interest seems to be in 'surrounding' or 'enclosing' various objects with the bands. An elastic band is already a closed shape as opposed to a line of string, which has the potential to form a line or a circle.

Harry appears to bring some of these ideas together when he is filmed at our house, aged 3 years 5 months:

> *'Harry is in the kitchen. He is holding one end of a long piece of string, which is already connected to a chair on the opposite side of the kitchen. He threads the end repeatedly through the handle of a low kitchen cupboard. When he has secured that end to the handle, by using up all of the loose string at that end, he moves across the kitchen and begins threading the loose string at the other end through another handle in a similar way. Georgia, who is playing nearby, goes to close the cupboard. Harry says, "No – they have to be open". As he plays, he says to his mum, "Mum – while we were coming back from Thomas the Tank, Mop drived at the Golf Club". Colette says "The Golf Club?" He goes on, "Yes – in the carpark of the Golf Club". Colette says, "In the carpark?"*

> *Harry continues, "Cos some people wanted to see in there". Harry gives a satisfied sigh, raises both arms in the air stretching his hands towards his mum and says, "The gate's done!" ' (video clip)*

Using a cognitive lens to understand Harry's play

We know that this is very important to Harry and that he is involved in 'deep level learning' because of his concentration, body language, attention to detail, obvious satisfaction and motivation to continue (Laevers 1997). He is clearly using a cluster of schemas – trajectory, rotation, enclosure and connection – at a symbolic level when he tells us that he has created 'a gate' (Athey 1990: 40). Harry has created something that looks like a gate. He seems to have in mind what gates look like and what are their common features. His remark to Georgia, "They have to be open", might be connected to his idea of what gates are. His conversation indicates that he is thinking about the trip to Thomas the Tank Engine where he has seen the rail crossing gates open and close at close quarters. Another possibility is that there is a connection between his recollection of the journey back from Thomas (at Peterborough) and his play with string. Might the securing of string at fixed points represent the stopping off points during a journey? Is he simultaneously connecting nursery and home by sharing his recollection of a nursery experience with his mum? Many of Harry's drawings look like string. Almost a year later, at 4 years 4 months, Harry draws two maps. One represents his dad's house and garden and the other his dad's journey to work.

Athey (1990) says that 'Representation provides evidence of "received" curriculum content' (p. 207). In other words, when children articulate what they are representing, we can be certain of their knowledge. Harry serves a long apprenticeship in learning about moving in lines (trajectory behaviour) and dropping off objects at certain points (transporting behaviour). He represents journeys in different ways, for example with small world cars, trains and blocks, before he reaches the stage of drawing the moving line that represents his dad's journey to work.

Using an emotional lens to understand Harry's play

Another explanation for using string to connect might be that Harry is representing his life in two homes with two parents. His play with

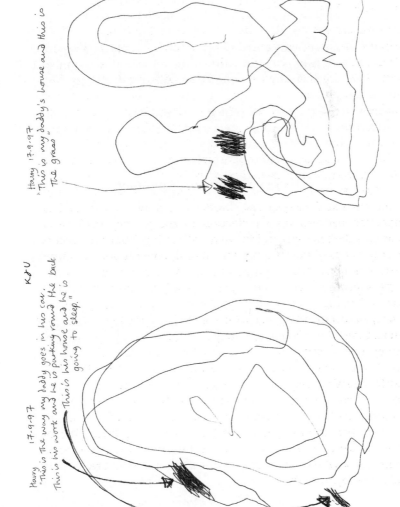

Harry 17·9·97   K & U
"This is the way my daddy goes in his car.
This is his work and he is parking round. He back.
This is his home and he is
going to sleep."

Harry 17·9·97
"This is my daddy's house and this is
the grass"

Figure 7.1 Harry draws two maps.

string might be a metaphor for his wish to connect his two lives. Winnicott (1990) tells us about a child who uses string obsessively. Winnicott's diagnosis is that the child needs an opportunity to talk through issues about separation. Perhaps Harry's cognitive interest in string and connection enables him to 'work through' some of his feelings about being connected/disconnected when adjusting to living in two homes.

Harry is also strongly exerting his power in his play. Using string to connect objects in different parts of the room and house make a huge statement about the importance of him and his freely chosen play. Although Harry also uses string to connect at nursery, he tends to use it to connect trailers to vehicles and this is often out of doors, where there is scope for using larger spaces for play and he does not, therefore, dominate the available space.

The role of others in Harry's creative play with string

During the same video clip, the play develops and we see Harry's clear interest in 'functional dependency relationships' (Athey 1990: 70). Harry has made another 'gate' and invites his mum into the living room to see all of the tying he has been doing. We now see Harry's creative thinking as he begins to focus on the functional aspects of having a gate between the kitchen and living room (Athey 1990: 69):

> 'Harry: "And look – a gate – so no big ones . . . you have to go under if them want to go past".
> Georgia: "Or you can step over".
> Colette: "Don't think I could even step over this – it's higher than the top of my leg".
> Harry: "Try!" '

Athey (1990) says that 'In early education "functional dependency relationships" are manifest when children observe the effects of action on objects or material' (p. 70). In this instance, Harry can see and judge that going from the kitchen to the living room would involve 'big ones' in going under. Georgia helps him to extend his thought by pointing out that 'big ones' might 'step over'. Colette further articulates the problem by pointing out that being able to step over depends on comparing the height of the gate with the length of her leg. Harry is excited by this idea and urges her to "Try!"

How Harry's explorations with string develop over time

Through his explorations with string, Harry discovers which objects are stable (like the kitchen cupboards) and which are moveable (like the kitchen stepladder). He realizes that he can make some objects move through the air by threading string through handles or enclosures and manipulating the string at either end. He does this with the lid of the laundry basket, scissors, a basket and a silver trophy. Other objects are too heavy for him to move through the air with string, but can be pulled along the floor from one location to another, for example, a wooden stool.

Harry's explorations become more refined: '*At 3 years 7 months Harry uses string to connect several small cars together in a line*'. At 3 years 8 months, he begins to make more realistic estimations about length: '*Harry had a ball of string and told his mum it would stretch "to Kettering" (5 miles). She commented, "That's a very long way". He revised his thinking, saying "It would go from Uncle Paul's house to here" (about a mile)*'. Towards the end of his year at nursery, Harry (aged 4 years 2 months) begins using string to tie groups of objects together, for example three highlighters or two cars. He also becomes interested in making a loop at one end of his string and moving objects on a vertical or horizontal plane.

Construction, role play and making models

Construction

Building is one of the ways in which Harry expresses his ideas. According to the parent diary, when he is 2 years 10 months, '*Harry is very interested in tunnels. He uses duplo tunnels, spots a tunnel in a book about the village of Geddington and is using arcs in the maple block area at drop-in*'. At first, he leans unit blocks against his structure to create a sort of tunnel. At this stage, Harry has had some first-hand experiences of going through tunnels but seems to be trying to work out how they are formed. He does not quite understand that, when using straight blocks, he needs two sides and one across the top to form a grid shape. It may not be a coincidence that on this occasion he has chosen to wear a checked shirt, which is a pattern made up of grid shapes. Then, at 3 years 1 month, Harry selects all of the arcs and arches to make a

Figure 7.2 Harry, aged 2 years 9 months, leans unit blocks against his building to create a tunnel.

tunnel and also constructs arches with three cylinders and a unit block. Harry also fetches the trainset, which is further evidence that he is representing tunnels.

Several months later, when Harry is 3 years 8 months, he and Georgia use an empty tissue box to represent a 'tunnel-like' shape over the train track of Grandpop's electric train. It has a hole at the top and flaps at each end: '*Harry covers the hole at the top with a piece of card and uses blu tack to secure it. He closes the flaps and secures them with blu tack. He calls the flaps "doors". Harry says "It's night time" and talks about Henry the Engine. Harry is excited and jumps up and down*'. His ideas develop as he explores the possibilities:

Figure 7.3 Harry, aged 3 years 1 month, selects arcs and arches and also constructs arches.

'Harry: *"That can be a shed for Thomas – when Thomas want to get out, me undo that and let him out"* and *"When it raining, he won't get wet"* Harry goes to the controls. *"Me driving Thomas".* He operates the switch and the movement of the train makes the *"doors"* burst open. Harry repeats this several times and laughs loudly each time. He also runs to the front of the shed to see it happening. He keeps repeating his actions saying, *"It's night time for him"* each time'. (video clip)

Using a cognitive lens to understand Harry's play with the train and shed

Harry seems to be very interested in the functional aspects of what happens. He enjoys making Thomas burst through the doors. The doors bursting open are functionally dependent on Harry operating the switch to make the train move forward (Athey 1990). The sequence of events is important. First, Harry explores and discovers what he can do with the materials he is using. Then, he builds a story around his actions and the objects he is using. Symbolic representation seems to follow functional dependency. Pahl (1999) talks about how boys' play is different from girls' play: 'While the girls tended to develop stories and then express their ideas in models . . . the boys would model in order to discover the story' (p. 90). She adds that 'Boys' stories tend to focus on action'. Harry creates a story by using characters he knows well (Thomas the Tank Engine and Friends), ideas he is trying to understand (darkness and night-time) and his own actions (operating the trainset). Bruce (1991: 59) would say that Harry is using several features of 'free-flow play'.

Harry engages in this play during the time that he wears his hood up almost constantly. The shed may also signify his understanding of going through a dark or difficult time and coming out of the other side. Isaacs (1952) talks about 2-year-olds, left at nursery for the first time, being comforted by playing with small objects and a post box. She says: 'The child thus seemed able to overcome his feelings of loss about his mother by means of this play, in which he lost and rediscovered objects at his own will' (p. 115). Harry, through his play, can create a scenario where Thomas is in the dark and he, Harry, enables him to move forward and burst through the doors into the light. This may have emotional significance for Harry. As adults, we talk about 'seeing the light at the end of the tunnel'. Maybe, at this time, Harry is beginning to see the light at the end of his tunnel.

Role play

We see Harry take part in role play scenarios, initiated by Georgia, as soon as he can crawl. Usually the play is around families and family events. When Harry is 1 year 6 months, they play *'going on holiday'* and work extremely hard carrying clothes, bags and toys from upstairs to downstairs. Often James, their nextdoor neighbour, joins in. They negotiate roles. Harry often wants to be the *'Dad'*, but is overruled by the two older children and has to make do with being the *'baby'* or the *'brother'*. Engels (1995) says that 'children organise experience into sequences; they experience the world as a series of events' (p. 28). So when children are engaging in family play, they are re-playing events in their lives, discovering how some of the other players feel and think. Gopnik *et al.* (1999) say that younger siblings learn more about other minds from their brother or sister than they do from their parents. This is possibly because the older brother or sister is less likely to do what a younger child wants. Therefore, the younger child has to work harder to 'try to understand their older sibling and to make predictions about them' (Gopnik *et al.* 1999: 57–8).

When Harry is 2 years 4 months, he is *'playing on the floor, crawling and being a "doggy". He pretends to bite each person's foot and says "Woo woo" '*. At this stage, Harry seems to be interested in experiencing the world from the physical position of being a dog. Pound (1999: 22) names 'orientation' as a schema or persistent concern of young children. The dictionary definition of 'orientation' is 'a relative position', so when Harry is being a dog, he is trying out viewing the objects and people around him from the position of a dog that is on all fours (Tulloch 1993).

Harry enjoys listening to stories and watching videos. The videos he watches turn out to be very important shared material when he starts nursery. When Harry is 3 years 10 months and he has been to the cinema to see '101 Dalmatians', he begins playing 'Lucky, the dog'. At first he plays alone and relates many of his experiences to being a dog or other animal. At home, aged 3 years 10 months: *'I gave Harry pasta bows for lunch. He said they were bones'*. At nursery, at the same age: *'Harry was inside the outdoor playhouse for 35 minutes alone. He kept opening the door and making "cross" faces. He told Lorna he was a uni-cow'*. On the way back from London Zoo that Easter, at 3 years 11 months:

> *'Harry was Lucky, Uncle Paul had to be Pongo and me the mummy. Harry (Lucky) whimpered and the mummy and daddy bared their teeth and growled. Then he was Scooby Doo and Paul had to be Shaggy (with a long neck). When we arrived home he crawled around the floor with my bag around his waist, saying he was a reindeer'.*

We see in Chapter 4 that Harry uses role play as a way of being in control of situations.

Making models

In the same way that Harry manipulates and tries things out with the tissue box, he enjoys manipulating and trying things out with paper or wood. When Harry makes a model, he is usually interested in its function. He manipulates paper, using sellotape, hole reinforcers or

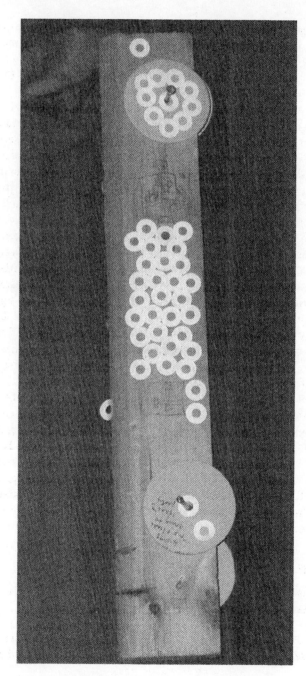

Figure 7.4 Harry's model of 'Me and Isaac going to Isaac's party'.

blu tack to join the paper together in different ways. He often decides what his model might be used for *after* he has made it. Examples are 'a mat to put your plate on' (aged 4 years 7 months), a pouch 'for putting money in' (5 years 11 months) and a 'pen carrier' (5 years 11 months).

At nursery, Harry frequently uses the woodwork bench. He saws, hammers and uses a hand drill. The end product is rarely of interest to him. After Harry starts school, he is still dropped off at nursery one day a week. He likes to stay and play and to chat with Maureen, the cleaner, who is a special person for many nursery children. He begins working on a model at nursery (after school), aged 5 years 1 month, and adds to it at home. At first his interest is in making a vehicle with wheels. At this stage, he is clear about his intentions but still open to things developing. Then, 4 months later, when he is very interested in enclosures, he adds hole reinforcers. He explains that *"bullets went through"*. Finally, 3 weeks later, he draws himself and his best friend at school, Isaac, *'going to Isaac's party'*. He draws windows on either side of the vehicle, through which he and Isaac can be seen. Each figure is facing outwards rather than showing a profile. Light and Barnes (1995) say this is usual up to about the age of 7. They say that children draw things 'as if to make them more easily recognisable' (p. 246); that is, include features that will communicate to others what they are representing.

Vygotsky (1978) points out that, 'Young children name their drawings only after they have completed them; they need to see them before they decide what they are' (p. 28). So this stage of trying things out and discovering the possibilities seems crucial if Harry is to be creative. Vygotsky adds, 'As children get older, they can decide in advance what they are going to draw'. At first, therefore, Harry explores the possibilities and sees what he can do with the materials he has. Then these possibilities become part of the repertoire he can use in a planned and thoughtful way.

Bringing ideas forward from earlier first-hand experiences

Occasionally, we can see where an idea has come from. On Christmas Day, when Harry is 2 years 7 months:

> *'Paul took Harry home to pick up his new car track. When they got back, Harry accidentally knocked the car key out of Paul's hand*

I am walking along with Paul.

and he knocked me in the drain and I fell into to the water.

2|10|98

and Paul knocked me down the drain. And he knocked me in the water.

Figure 7.5 Harry's drawings and story about Paul knocking him down the drain.

and it fell down the drain. We spent ages trying to retrieve the key. Georgia and Harry were very excited. We tried using a large magnet and various contraptions to hook the key. Eventually we succeeded'.

More than two and a half years later, when Harry is 5 years 4 months, he does some drawings and dictates a story about Paul knocking him down the drain and into the water. He seems to be using what he learned much earlier to create a story into which he incorporates the concept of 'falling down a drain and into the water'.

Summary

In this chapter, we have been considering:

- what creativity is;
- how Harry expresses his ideas through using different materials and objects;
- how Harry's play develops over time;
- what Harry may be thinking and feeling when he is being creative;
- the concepts Harry is trying to understand when he is being creative.

Table 7.1 Schemas mentioned in Chapter 7

Lines
Seriation
Grid
One-to-one correspondence
Enclosure
Connection
Trajectory
Rotation
Going through a boundary
Envelopment
Orientation
Transporting

In the next chapter, we explore how Harry gains further knowledge and understanding of the world.

8 Harry gains further knowledge and understanding of the world

Throughout this book so far, we have been considering how Harry gains knowledge and understanding of his world. We see that he does this by being curious, asking questions and exploring; through getting to know the people that he encounters; and through investigating the properties of objects and materials he comes across. The *Curriculum Guidance for the Foundation Stage* (QCA 2000) (the English Early Years Curriculum) defines 'Knowledge and Understanding' as having five aspects:

1   Exploration and investigation
2   Designing and making skills
3   A sense of time
4   A sense of place
5   Cultures and beliefs

The Curriculum Guidance emphasizes the importance of 'first-hand experiences that encourage exploration, observation, problem solving, prediction, critical thinking, decision making and discussion' (p. 82).

Loris Malagussi (in Edwards *et al.* 1998: 3) talks about the child:

> The child has
> A hundred languages . . .
> A hundred ways of thinking
> of playing, of speaking . . .

Harry, like every other child, finds his own ways to understand his world, to satisfy his curiosity and to create new knowledge for himself. In this chapter, we see how Harry progresses towards a wider understanding of the world.

The chapter is divided into sections:

- Learning about growth and development through his own history
- Exploring how he can make things happen
- Gaining a sense of time and place
- Designing and making models
- Making links with the wider world

Learning about growth and development through his own history

We saw in Chapter 2 that Harry (aged 2 years 8 months) is puzzled when he sees Uncle Paul's cat as a tiny kitten and then as a cat. He deduces that *'Uncle Paul must have two cats – a little one and a bigger one'*. It is clear that, at this stage, he does not accept the explanation that the kitten has grown up and looks different.

Harry learns about himself as a baby

The records show that Harry has been interested in himself, Georgia and other babies for several months:

- At 1 year 9 months, *'says "Baby" and fetches photo from hall table'*.
- At 1 year 10 months, *'pretends to be a baby, crawling on "all fours" '*.
- At 1 year 10 months, *'watches a video of Georgia, as a one year old, and says "Dorda" '*.
- At 1 year 11 months, *'carries a photo of himself, as a baby, saying "Baby" and "me" '*.
- At 1 year 11 months and 2 years 1 month, *'plays with dolls and buggies and feeds "babies" '*.
- At 2 years 4 months, when he watches a Pingu video, *'one of his favourite bits is "the babies". He talks about "baby crying" '*.

- At 2 years 7 months, *'visiting his great grandmother, he says "Nanny me baby" – we think he means "Nanny thinks I'm a baby". He knows he is not a baby'.*

At this stage, Harry can 'assimilate' the information that he and Georgia were both babies once and that now they are not babies. However, he cannot yet 'accommodate' the steps from baby to child or kitten to cat (Piaget 2001). Over a period of time Harry becomes interested in identifying everyone on family photos even when they are obviously a lot younger and look very different.

Harry begins to reflect on his own life. When he is 3 years 2 months, he and Georgia are painting: *'Colette said "It's interesting that Harry has always liked the colour orange". Harry reflects "Even when me two"'.* Harry may be thinking about what stays the same despite a change in age label. Later that day at the supermarket, *'Harry kept commenting on what he is "allowed" to eat, "not milk or cheese but eggs". He says "Me like eggs"'.* Now he seems to be thinking about what changes as he grows older and stronger. For a long time, Harry is not allowed eggs because of an allergy but, after a test of his tolerance, he is now allowed eggs.

Harry continues to explore ideas about growth and development, mostly through conversations. On Paul's birthday, when Harry is 3 years 4 months: *'Harry is interested in babies and in how little he was. He laughs when I say "Paul used to be a tiny, tiny baby"'.* At 3 years 5 months, Harry talks about the future: *"When me be 5, me go to school" and "Georgia's 5 and she goes to school and gymnastics"'.*

How Harry begins to gain a clearer understanding about growth

When Harry is 3 years 8 months: *'Harry asked for the video "Me when me a baby" on. He noticed that his skin and hair were dark when he was a tiny baby. He watched it for a long time'.* He watches this video of himself, aged 2 weeks to 2 years, many times over the next year. The video shows his incremental growth and change over time.

Harry begins to reflect on and trace his own development. At 3 years 11 months, he recalls something from the video: *'Harry looked in the garden at the yellow broom (in full bloom). I said that the lavender will be out soon – Harry reflected on what he had seen on video – himself aged one year picking the flowers and me saying "Don't pick the flowers*

Harry" but he still did'. At 4 years 4 months, Harry reflects on a skill he has developed: *'On the way home, Harry was talking to Paul about being able to whistle – "When I was 2 I couldn't whistle" and "when I was 3 I learnt to whistle", then he demonstrated'*. Harry is beginning to associate age with development.

It may be coincidental but, during the time that Harry is reflecting on himself, as a baby and in the future, he is also very interested in ladders. He talks about ladders, finds ladders in stories and uses mobilo to make a vehicle *'with a long, extending ladder'*. The ladder may provide Harry with a kind of metaphor or symbol for understanding how time passes and growth and development occur. Each step or rung of the ladder may represent an increment or small change in appearance or size. Harry is trying to understand the process of growth and change. Being able to capture the small changes, like snapshots, one on each rung of a ladder, may be helping Harry to think about connecting up the stages into a moving picture of living and growing.

Pahl (1999: 21) talks about how the models that children make reflect their ideas:

> Using one idea, the children are driven by internal links within them to explore other possibilities . . . If an object reminds children of something else, they are able to develop it structurally so that it becomes the thing inside their heads. The meanings change and grow inside their minds.

Harry is not making models but may be searching for models in the environment that help him to think about growth and change. Bruce *et al.* (1995: 37) tell us that Froebel talks about making the inner/outer and outer/inner. They quote Gurland (Bruce *et al.* 1995: 40), who says:

> Froebel, we remember, spoke in rather mystical terms of the relation of the 'inner' and the 'outer' that is, of an internal, personal world which seeks expression by projecting itself into the outer world through creative activities and an outer, external world which has to be understood and accepted and made part of the personal world through a mastery of its laws and characteristics. This interpretation of the external reality and the personal inner world depends on seeing relation-

ships, making links: it needs an intellectual activity of understanding and adaptation.

Might Harry be seeing a link between what he is trying to understand and the ladder?

Harry explores ideas about family roles, life and death

When Harry is 3 years 8 months, he is playing at '*being daddy*'. We can gain insights into what his real daddy does from his role play:

> '*He is cutting up elastic and ribbon into small pieces and putting the bits into sieves (3 sizes). Gives dinner to himself – the biggest ("because I am the daddy"), Pop and me. He says of Georgia, "If you don't know her name, just call her 'Mummy' ". Said he was going to work "at 9" and would be back "about 2". Looked up and said "It's raining", then "if it's raining, me go in the car" and "if it's not, me just walk" *'.

Here Harry is demonstrating his understanding of *why* his daddy might have the biggest meal and of *why* he might go in the car as opposed to walking.

Gradually, over time, Harry's ideas about growth and development become clearer. However, he still has some questions. At 4 years 6 months:

> '*I was talking about when his mummy, her brother and sister were children and we went camping. Harry asked, "Was I in my mummy's tummy then?" I said "No, that was before that". Harry: "Was I in my daddy's tummy then?" I began explaining that children cannot have babies and that bodies change, etc. Harry said, "Only ladies can have babies" *'.

On reflection, I think Harry is asking a deeper question about where life begins. In a way, it is logical to think that if he is not in his mummy's tummy, then he must be in his daddy's tummy. Whether Harry understands or not, the potential to have a baby depends on both parents. He may have a sense of this and because he cannot imagine life without Harry, he naturally wants to know *where* he is.

Thinking about where and when life begins seems to lead Harry to thinking about when and how life ends. At 4 years 9 months: '*Was at my house with Paul – had told Paul that the rectangles on the rug look like "coffins with the lids closed"* '. Two days later:

> '*We were going to Kettering by car – we reached the roundabout near Danesholme and Harry said "People who aren't old can die if their car crashes".*
> *Me: "Yes – that's what happened to my sister – she was in a car crash and died".*
> *Harry: "What was her name?"*
> *Me: "Angela".*
> *Harry: "Were you grown up?"*
> *Me: "Yes I was".*
> *Harry: "Was she younger than you?"*
> *Me: "She was 17 – yes, younger than me".*
> *Harry: "What happened?" and "How do people die?"*
> *Me: "Well – she went to sleep for 10 days and then stopped breathing – that's what happens when people die – they stop breathing".*

Harry seems to be satisfied with that explanation.

When Harry is 4 years 11 months, he is looking at a photograph book of himself as a toddler and refers to himself as '*Tinky Winky*'. He is astute in recognizing the toddler-like appearance of the Teletubby character. A month later, when he is 5 years old:

> '*A man walking a dog was approaching. Harry held back, wary of the dog. I said "It's a Spaniel like Daddy used to have". Harry said "Snoopy was a very good dog. It died and went to heaven – that's where animals go when they die". Georgia: "They go in graves". Harry: "Yes – they go in graves"* '.

Snoopy dies before either of the children are born, so Harry's ideas about Snoopy are from conversations with his parents.

When Harry is 5 and the children are staying overnight: '*Harry brought the Hercules video and told me that Hercules was a baby at the beginning and grew into a man*'. Watching the Hercules video seems to help Harry to consolidate his ideas. He can now hold in mind a moving picture of the growth and development of humans and animals.

Exploring how he can make things happen

We see in Chapter 1 that Harry likes to twiddle the knobs and buttons on his dad's stereo. At this stage, he seems interested in the movement rather than the effect.

Harry explores going through a boundary

When Harry is 2 years 3 months, he seems interested in the effect of his actions. He is using a pump action container of cream: *'All Harry was interested in was pressing the pump and catching the cream on his hand – at first he could not coordinate his movements. He did not realize that one hand needed to be under the spout. He got the hang of it eventually'*. To make this happen, Harry has to coordinate several schemas. Harry is using an *up/down dynamic trajectory* schema to make the cream *go through the boundary* of the tube and is *positioning* his hand 'palm up' under the spout so that the cream will land *on top* of his hand (Athey 1990). The cream is *inside* the container and reaches the *outside* because of Harry's action.

At 2 years 4 months: *'Harry got the small hoover and began hoovering the carpet. Got Teddy Tim and put his paw on the handle of the hoover, then did the same with Teddy Tom'*. Harry can see bits of paper or dust going from *outside* the container to *inside* (the opposite to the cream). He can feel the suction but cannot see it. The hoover he is using is a small hand-held rechargeable hoover. At first he uses it until it runs out of power completely. This puzzles him. Gradually he learns that the hoover will only run for a certain amount of time until it needs recharging on its place on the wall. So, somehow, the hoover *contains* power that goes from *inside* to *outside*. It cannot be seen but can be heard.

At 3 years of age: *'Harry got his tape measure out, extended it and held it up like a sword. What he was most interested in was using the switch and saying "open" and "shut" as he changed it (it's a bit like a lock or dam to stop the tape going through)'*. The tape measure can come out and go back and, therefore, demonstrates 'reversibility'. Athey (1990: 41) says that:

> Operational thought has certain characteristics, such as 'reversibility', which is essential for 'conservation'. For the stable mathematical operation of *addition*, the mental action

of grouping together must be able to be cancelled out by reversing the process . . . *Subtraction* cancels *addition* . . .

With the tape measure, Harry can extend it and see more, retract it and see less, so there is an addition and subtraction of length. The tape *going through* (either way) is 'functionally dependent' on Harry pushing or pulling it (Athey 1990: 70). When he holds it up, he may be symbolically representing a sword.

Exploring 'going through a boundary' with different objects seems to help Harry (aged 3 years 3 months) to conceptualize and to think about 'going through' a boundary that he cannot see. He demonstrates this ability when he makes an important connection. I was talking about being at Corby Golf Club:

> '*Harry: "Where?"*
> *Me: "Corby – you've been there – we've had dinner there". In my*
> *effort to explain, I said "Where the rabbits are".*
> *Harry: "In the holes?"*
> *Me: "Yes, that's where they live in tunnels under the ground".*
> *Harry very quickly said, "We've got cable TV!" '*

Here Harry seems to be seeing a similarity between the tunnels made by rabbits under the ground and the cables laid underground to pipe in cable television. In seeing the similarity, Harry can 'assimilate' the idea of the underground cables carrying signals or messages to the television screen.

Harry moves objects through space

Aged 3 years 3 months: '*Harry threads string through the handle of the kitchen cupboard and then the handle of the laundry basket lid – he enjoyed making the door open and moving the lid along the line of string*'. At this stage, he seems to be 'exploring' what happens when he connects fixed and moveable objects together with string and then moves the string (Bruce 1991). Having 'discovered' that he can move objects through space: '*Harry (3 years 5 months) threaded a piece of string through a bobbin. A bit later, he threaded a piece of string through the finger holes of a pair of scissors, then put the string through the handle of a cupboard door and pulled the string to lift the scissors*'. Now Harry seems to have a definite plan of how to move objects through space. At nursery between 3 years 4 months and 4 years 3 months, Harry frequently uses the two pulleys to move objects up and down.

Harry coordinates his ideas

When Harry is 3 years 11 months, he coordinates his ideas about direction, going through a boundary and functional dependency when he is playing with Pop's electric trainset. He is operating the train by using a switch. He can make it go forward/reverse and stop/slow/fast:

> *'Pop had put a single loop (enclosure) of track out. Harry got out a level crossing and played for a while running the train around the track, stopping and opening the gate manually. Then, I'm not sure whether it was by chance or plan, the gate was slightly open and the impact of the moving train opened the gate'.*

So this is one thing that Harry learns by doing it. He can make one gate open with the moving train. *'However, as both gates open by being pushed from opposite directions, the moving train could open one but not the other. In fact it would crash into the second gate if it continued moving'.* This is the second thing that Harry learns: if the train continues moving, it will crash into the second gate.

> *'After much persistence and practice, Harry discovered that he could open one gate by propelling the train forward but, to open the second gate, he had to reverse the train all around the track so that it impacted against the second gate by pushing it. He was very excited when that worked and he did that several times and also the next morning'.*

Harry is demonstrating how he can coordinate a complex set of ideas to solve a problem that he has set himself. This links with some of Harry's explorations into his 'sense of place' in the next section.

Gaining a sense of time and place

Harry gains a sense of time

We have seen how Harry begins to differentiate between past, present and future time throughout the book. Bancroft (1995) says that 'An understanding of "time" in the sense used by Piaget involves understanding the notions of "duration" and "sequencing" rather than the ability to tell the time or to know the order of days and months' (p. 140).

We see in Chapter 5 that Harry counts and waits when he is playing hide and seek. He is spending a length of time counting and waiting so that the other children can hide. In Chapter 6, we see that Harry uses a kitchen timer so that he and Georgia can have equal amounts of time playing with Pop's electric trainset. In this chapter, we have been hearing about Harry's gradual understanding of how growth and development link with time. At nursery at 3 years 8 months: *'Harry seems to be interested in greater or less time. "Me be really bwick [quick], 1 minute or 3 minutes or 2 minutes". Then he runs fast to the office and back'*. Harry is racing to make his journey in the least time possible.

In the records, there are several references to Harry's interest in the moon, night-time and darkness. Like other young children, day and night are probably the first divisions of time of which Harry becomes aware. At 3 years 4 months: *'Harry talked about people working at night. He said "My daddy works at night – 2 nights outside London – that not a long time"'*. He is thinking about the duration of his dad's work outside London. At the age of 4, Harry notices that the moon is out on the way home (it is still light). Harry has two ideas: *"Might be it likes to be out in the light"* or *"Might be it thinks it's still night"*. Neither idea seems to link with time. Piaget (1962) says that young children go through a stage of attributing intentionality to the sun, moon and other objects. He refers to this as 'animism'. Piaget gives the example of J (aged 5 years 6 months), who says: 'The moon's hiding in the cloud again. It's cold' (p. 251).

When Harry is 5 years 2 months, he begins to realize that time effects others while it is effecting him: *'Harry chatted about his age and what ages he will be in future, for example, 6 up to 10. Mentioned Georgia's age relative to his, for example, "When I am 15 Georgia will be 17"'*. This shows that Harry can conceptualize time moving forward.

Harry gains a sense of place

Harry begins to gain a 'sense of place' through his early transporting behaviour, when he embarks on journeys and carries objects, displacing them with different people in different places (see Chapter 1).

Later on, we hear that he marks some of his journeys with string. He represents journeys symbolically when he plays with trains and tracks. Over a long period of time, Harry (aged 3 years 8 months to 6 years) plays a game on the computer called 'Rover' which involves taking a dog through a maze using the directional arrows. The game is played at 38 increasingly difficult levels. At nursery, we look at a map of the local area. Harry likes to roll his map up.

Harry begins to gain a general sense of direction and of where places are in relation to each other (see Chapter 6). One journey that Harry makes many times and that seems to intrigue him is from our back gate to front door. (This seems to link with Harry's play with the electric trainset referred to earlier in this chapter.) We live in a mid-terrace house. We have a back gate and, to go from there to the front door, you have to go along a narrow path into the close behind our road, around in a circle, past several houses to the front. (It is not obvious.) The records show that:

- Harry (aged 4 years 3 months) '*came to our house with his bike – rode around from front into back gate*'.
- Harry (aged 5 years) '*asked if I would go around the block and in the back gate with him and Georgia. I did, then Pop did, then mummy did. They then had a couple of goes each doing that alone before they went home*'.
- Four days later: '*When Ian came, Harry wanted to walk around Squire Close and in the back gate like he did on Wednesday. Both children had one turn before leaving*'.
- On the evening of a family party, when Harry is 5 years 2 months, '*he spent most of the evening racing adults from the back gate to the front door*'.
- At 5 years 10 months: '*Pop and I are back from our holiday in India today. Pop was explaining about the husk of the coconut being spun into rope, so I fetched the coconut and rope to show them. Harry immediately wanted to hold one end of rope and someone to hold the other end and to walk around the block. Georgia held the other end*'.

These investigations seem to link with his interest in the underground map on a trip to London 3 weeks later: '*Harry (aged 5 years 11 months) is interested in the map of London Underground. He wants to know where we are on the map. He can see that the train travels in a circle*'.

Designing and making models

Another strand running through the records is Harry's interest in making models from paper or wood (see Chapter 7). When Harry is 4 years 7 months and the children have been staying overnight, they spend all morning making paper aeroplanes and trying them out: *'Harry lines his planes up right across the living room. He begins writing his name and a number on each one. He says that number 1 goes the farthest. He likes standing on the arm of an armchair to launch his planes' (video clip).* Some of the time Harry copies what Georgia does, for example, folding the corners in and sellotaping them. He can cut the sellotape with the scissors in either hand. He gives some of his models a *function* after making them, for example *"A mat for the table – for having your dinner on"*.

There has been some research on how children draw three-dimensional objects in two dimensions (Light and Barnes 1995: 240). What we notice is that Harry explores making two-dimensional paper into three-dimensional shapes first.

Two weeks after making aeroplanes, Harry (aged 4 years 8 months) *'made a "hat" by sellotaping 2 sheets of A4 paper together'*. The next day:

> *'said I had given him "a good idea" about how to make a "house". He folded a piece of A4 paper in half and placed it like an upside-down V. It was not very strong so I suggested making a triangle to strengthen each end – I drew a triangle the right size by tracing the shadow of the V – Harry cut it out and stuck it to the V with sellotape'.*

At 5 years 2 months: *'Harry and Georgia used old curtains, a clothes horse and pegs to make a tent in the garden. His concern was with balance and symmetry'.* When Harry is 5 years 4 months:

> *'I haven't actually seen Harry do this, but around the kitchen are several enclosures – 3 pieces of rolled up paper, which have been sellotaped along the edge; a photo frame with an elastic band around it; a bottle of sun cream with an elastic band around it; and a rolled up piece of paper with an elastic band around it twice'.*

Figure 8.1 Harry incorporates enclosures in his drawing, for example, earrings and nostrils.

Soon after making these enclosures, Harry (aged 5 years 5 months) incorporates enclosures into his drawing.

Harry explores transforming two dimensions into three-dimensional models before attempting to draw three-dimensional objects. When he is 5 years 6 months, he draws the design of something he wants me to help him make – a sword.

Making links with the wider world

Harry continues to pursue his home interests during his first year at school. It is only during his second year at school that we notice

Figure 8.2 Harry's design of what he wants me to help him make – a sword.

his school interests having a major impact on what Harry does at home.

Harry's world extends

Just after the beginning of his second year at school, when he is 5 years 4 months, Harry is making observations and asking questions about 'the world': *'Harry's world seems to have suddenly extended. On the way home he was talking about "the world" and saying "the sun is following me" and "how can the sun warm the whole country when it is a very long way away?"'* Harry talks about a new experience he has had through making a new friend, who lives in a village outside Corby:

'He spoke about "Great Easton and Great Easton Hall" (where his friend, Isaac, had his birthday party). He said that when he went to Isaac's for tea, he ate all of the food – "It was potatoes and chicken and corn on the cob" '.

Coordinating earlier ideas

Harry coordinates several of his earlier ideas when he (aged 5 years 5 months) and Georgia play raffles:

> 'He only understood it when he actually did it. Even then, he tried to rig it so that we all got a turn at winning. He and Georgia would each draw a picture, then sell each member of the family a numbered ticket. Then they would place a corresponding numbered ticket in a bowl. Finally, one person would draw out a ticket and Harry would announce the winner of each drawing'.

Georgia soon loses interest but Harry wants to repeat the process over and over again. The game goes on for several weeks. He would draw or paint something very quickly *in order to* raffle it. The element of surprise seems important to Harry, although he tries to ensure that each person has a turn at winning.

What Harry needs to know to organize a raffle

Harry seems to want to practise holding raffles because he has only just managed to remember all of the steps in the procedure. Several schemas are coordinated. A numbered ticket represents each of the participants. So there is a 'one-to-one correspondence' between people and tickets (Athey 1990: 192). Then there is a further 'one-to-one correspondence' between the tickets in the bowl and the tickets held by the participants. One set of tickets is 'spread out' or 'distributed' and the other set is 'heaped' (as in earlier 'transporting' behaviour). The sets are 'equivalent' to each other (Athey 1990: 35). The tickets are 'contained' in the bowl and the winner is hidden or 'enveloped' until the draw is made. In fact, the winner is enveloped in two layers; that is, first a number is drawn and then the person holding that numbered ticket identifies him or herself. The ticket drawn and the prize signify the winner. Numbering the tickets involves 'seriation' (Athey 1990: 41). Harry is also dealing with ratios –

that is, if five people are participating, each has a one-in-five chance of winning.

The school curriculum influences Harry's play at home

At 5 years 5 months, Harry becomes very interested in the theme of 'Light and Dark' that his class is exploring at school: *'Harry wanted to take something about "light" to school. He asked Georgia for her torch – she said "No". So he chose candles and holders, wrapped them in tissues, placed them in a shoe box and placed the box in a bag'*. We wonder why Harry envelops the candles in three layers of covering. Maybe there is a link between these layers and the layers hiding the identity of the winner of the raffle?

At 5 years 6 months, Harry paints lots of 'light and dark' pictures (using black, brown and white paint) and, again, raffles them:

> *'Did not sell tickets but asked each person what number they would like. He gave each person two tickets. He painted enough paintings for everyone to win at least one. He would paint one, raffle it, then paint the next one. Towards the end of his play, he picked up a paintbrush and said "This is wider – it'll be quicker". All of the paintings were about "day and night" or "sun and rain" '.*

A few days later: *'Harry arrived for dinner with a torch. Lit all of our candles (about 7 in various candlesticks) for the second time. Painted night time and day time pictures. Says he is going to be an artist when he grows up'.*

Harry's sense of fair play extends to others

We see in Chapter 4 that when Harry's security is threatened, he appears to need more than his fair share or to be first. Generally, he has a sense of what is fair and questions unfair treatment. Sometimes even now, aged 9 years, he tells us about unfair decisions made by his teacher.

When Harry is 5 years 8 months, he tells his mum about another child: *'Harry said Danielle had been "grounded" for eating a biscuit when she wasn't supposed to. Colette asked, "What do you think children should get grounded for?" Harry replied, "Breaking tables ... breaking picture frames ... breaking houses" (obviously trying to think of major things)'.*

Harry seems to be intimating that the punishment is too severe for the crime in this instance. He seems to be comparing his family culture with the cultures of other children he knows.

Summary

In this chapter, we have been considering:

- how Harry learns about the world through his own past;
- some examples of how Harry coordinates his movements and uses string to make things happen;
- what helps Harry to gain a sense of time and place;
- how Harry explores making two-dimensional shapes into three-dimensional models before drawing three-dimensional figures in two dimensions;
- how school and the wider world begin to impact on Harry's thinking.

Table 8.1   Schemas mentioned in Chapter 8

Line (history)
Grid
Going through a boundary
Up/down trajectory
Positioning
On top
Inside
Outside
Enclosure
Directions
One-to-one correspondence
Transporting
Containment
Envelopment
Layering
Seriation

In the final chapter, we reflect on Harry now, aged 9 years.

9 Reflections

We have been considering, throughout this book, how Harry explores all areas of learning through following his individual interests. In this final chapter, we look briefly at Harry's interests now, aged 9, and we consider what we have learned, from observing Harry, that we can use to understand other children's development and learning.

Harry's interests now aged 9

Harry says he enjoys

- playing football (he plays in a local team and trains two or three times a week)
- Playstation 2
- playing golf (goes to the driving range once a week)
- Charades
- Scrabble
- ten pin bowling (goes occasionally)
- Air hockey (a kind of executive pinball game).

Colette says that there are many obvious links between Harry's strong connecting schema and his current interests. He connects with other people through playing team games. He physically connects with the objects used in sports. He plays 'Charades' and 'Scrabble' at every opportunity. Here he is finding connections between words or phrases. He continues to create opportunities to solve problems. She says he is still *"very much his own person"* but that he *"takes others into account"*. Recently, Colette had a cold. Harry wanted to sleep in her bed but she persuaded him not to because she did not want him to catch her cold. When she went up to bed, she discovered he had put two of his soft toy dogs in her bed *"to look after her"*. Colette recognizes and appreciates that Harry and Georgia have been able to rely on each other throughout some difficult times in their lives. Like any other siblings, they fight and argue but their attachment to each other seems to have helped them.

Ian says that what he notices is that Harry still has the ability to be very focused and to concentrate for hours. When he uses his Playstation, he particularly enjoys games that involve strategic thinking. He likes playing a Football Manager Game, in which he has to buy players, manage the funding, coaching and all aspects of the game. Recently, he said to his Dad, *"I'm not going to spend all of my money on expensive players. I'm going to get a really good coach and he will bring the young players on"*. Harry says that he likes *"choosing the team formation so that he has a better team out"*. Ian says that Harry is also good at *"reading the game"* when he is playing. He will still occasionally get 'Connex' or 'Lego' out and, again, be very focused on making complex models.

What we have learned from observing Harry

Through closely observing Harry, we have learned many things that might help other parents and workers to understand and promote the interests of other children:

1   It is very valuable to have open-ended resources freely available at home and at nursery, for example, string, sellotape, blu tack, elastic bands, glue.
2   Harry experiments with making two-dimensional paper into three-dimensional shapes. Elastic bands provide the means with which he can hold the paper temporarily in place. We wonder if other children go from two to three dimensions before designing in two dimensions?
3   It is important to offer Harry the freedom to explore materials in his own way. He seems to become deeply involved and focused and creates his own problems to solve.
4   Harry appears to discover stories through his exploration of materials and drawing on his own first-hand experiences.

'How things work' and 'making things happen' seem to be his starting points.

5   Harry seems to express his inner fears when using soft toys.

6   Harry appears to discover and to use metaphors for concepts he is struggling to understand, for example, trains and track as a metaphor for past and future time.

7   Anything that puzzles Harry is important new learning for him and for us. We must treat his questions with respect and allow him to challenge our thinking.

8   When Harry is deeply involved, he is often exploring emotional issues as well as cognitive concerns.

9   Strategies that were helpful to Harry when he was emotionally vulnerable because of his parents' separation were: naming how he might be feeling; involving him and Georgia in choosing and physically moving their toys from one home to the other; and taking photographs in both homes. The focus on the process of moving and creating opportunities to talk about what was happening seemed to help Harry to understand and to cope.

How Harry expresses himself now

As a young child, Harry's speech is unclear and he uses immature speech forms. We have tried to quote him in his own words throughout the book, so that the reader can see when he makes progress. However, there are times when we simply could not understand what Harry was trying to tell us. On these occasions, Colette says it helped to acknowledge his feelings about not being understood, for example, say to him *"You must be feeling really frustrated that I can't understand you"*. Sometimes, as a family, we would adopt Harry's version of a word. This just seemed to happen and was in no way belittling to him. An example is 'orange juice' which Harry called *"baby odinge"* for a time. Even now, we refer to orange juice as *'baby odinge'*. I would say that every aspect of Harry's personality is valued and adopting his words is rather like admiring what makes Harry different.

It is quite difficult to offer a glimpse of the whole picture when relying on the written word. Harry has a really good sense of humour and can be witty. At Christmas just gone, when the children are putting out the usual snack for Santa (mince pies, milk and carrots for the reindeer), Harry suddenly pipes up, *"What if he's lactose intolerant!?"*

This year, on Mother's Day, Harry's class are shown an example and asked to write poems to their mothers. This is what Harry wrote:

> *'My mum is the best mum in the Galaxy.*
> *She is the best at making cookies.*
> *Her best cookies are chocolate chip ones.*
> *They are the best in the street.*
> *She makes me smile when I'm sad.*
> *And makes stupid jokes (that are not funny).*
> *My mum loves plants.*
> *My mum is the best.*
> *From Harry.'*

Colette says:

> *"What makes this poem so funny and so poignant is that he is right about everything – that is, we did make cookies, I do love plants and it is an ongoing joke that he thinks my jokes aren't funny!!"*

Miell, D. (1995) Developing a sense of self, in P. Barnes (ed.) *Personal, Social and Emotional Development of Children*. Buckingham: Open University Press.

Miller, L., Rustin, M., Rustin, M. and Shuttleworth, J. (eds) (1989) *Closely Observed Infants*. London: Duckworth.

Miller, P.H. (1995) a reading from *Theories of Developmental Psychology* (1989), in V. Lee and P. Das Gupta (eds) *Children's Cognitive and Language Development*. Buckingham: Open University Press.

Moll, L. C. (ed.) (1990, reprinted 1994), *Vygotsky and Education*. Cambridge: Cambridge University Press.

Navarra, J.G. (1955) *The Development of Scientific Concepts in a Young Child: A Case Study*. New York: Colombia University Press.

Nutbrown, C. (1994, 1999) *Threads of Thinking*. London: Paul Chapman.

Oates, J. (ed.) (1994) *The Foundations of Child Development*. Oxford: Blackwell.

Pahl, K. (1999) *Transformations: Meaning Making in Nursery Education*. Stoke-on-Trent: Trentham Books.

Pascal, C. and Bertram, A.D. (1977) *Effective Early Learning*. London: Hodder & Stoughton.

Pen Green Portfolios (2000) *Learning through Superhero Play, Pokemon Play*. Corby, Northants: Pen Green Centre.

Piaget, J. (1959a) *The Construction of Reality in the Child*. New York: Basic Books.

Piaget, J. (1959b) *The Language and Thought of the Child*, 3rd edn. London: Routledge.

Piaget, J. (1962) *Play, Dreams and Imitation in Childhood*. London: Routledge & Kegan Paul.

Piaget, J. (1980) *Adaptation and Intelligence*. Chicago, IL: University of Chicago Press.

Piaget, J. (2001) *The Psychology of Intelligence*. London: Routledge.

Pinker, S. (1994) *The Language Instinct*. London: Penguin.

Pollard, A. (1996) *The Social World of Children's Learning*. London: Cassell.

Pound, L. (1999) *Supporting Mathematical Development in the Early Years*. Buckingham: Open University Press.

Qualifications and Curriculum Authority (2000) *Curriculum Guidance for the Foundation Stage*. London: QCA.

Qualifications and Curriculum Authority (2001) *Planning for Learning in the Foundation Stage*. London: QCA.

Quinton, D. and Rutter, M. (1988) *Parenting Breakdown: The Making and Breaking of Inter-generational Links*. Aldershot: Avebury.

References

Arnold, C. (1997) Understanding young children and their contexts for learning and development: building on early experience. Unpublished master's dissertation, University of Leicester.

Arnold, C. (1999) *Child Development and Learning 2–5 Years: Georgia's Story*. London: Paul Chapman.

Athey, C. (1990) *Extending Thought in Young Children: A Parent–Teacher Partnership*. London: Paul Chapman.

Bancroft, D. (1995) Language development, in V. Lee and P. Das Gupta (eds) *Children's Cognitive and Language Development*. Buckingham: Open University Press.

Barnes, P. (ed.) (1995) *Personal, Social and Emotional Development of Young Children*. Buckingham: Open University Press.

Bartholomew, L. and Bruce, T. (1993) *Getting to Know You: A Guide to Record-keeping in Early Childhood Education and Care*. Sevenoaks: Hodder & Stoughton.

Blakemore, C. (1998) Talk on 'The brain', Pen Green Centre, Corby, Northants, November.

Boden, M.A. (1979) *Piaget*. Brighton: Harvester Press.

Borowski, E.J. and Borwein, J.M. (1989) *Collins Dictionary of Mathematics*. Glasgow: HarperCollins.

Bowlby, J. (1953) *Child Care and the Growth of Maternal Love*. London: Penguin.

Bowlby, J. (1969) *Attachment and Loss, Vol. 1: Attachment*. London: Pimlico.

Bowlby, J. (1998) *Separation: Anger and Anxiety*. London: Pimlico.

Browne, A. (1999) Developing writing, in J. Marsh and E. Hallett (eds) *Desirable Literacies*. London: Paul Chapman.

Bruce, T. (1991) *Time to Play in Early Childhood Education*. London: Hodder & Stoughton.

Bruce, T. (1997) *Early Childhood Education*. London: Paul Chapman.

Bruce, T. (2001) *Learning through Play*. London: Hodder & Stoughton.

Bruce, T. and Meggitt, C. (1996) 1st edn (1999) 2nd edn. *Child Care and Education*. London: Hodder & Stoughton.

Bruce, T., Findlay, A., Read, J. and Scarborough, M. (1995) *Recurring Themes in Education*. London: Paul Chapman.

Bruner, J. (1990) *Acts of Meaning*. London: Harvard University Press.

Carr, M. (2001) *Assessment in Early Childhood Settings*. London: Paul Chapman.

Chess, S. and Thomas, A. (1984) *Origins and Evolution of Behaviour Disorders*. New York: Brunner Mazel.

Cohen, D. (1983) *Piaget: Critique and Reassessment*. New York: St. Martin's Press.

Csikszentmihalyi, M. (1996) *Creativity Flow and the Psychology of Discovery and Invention*. New York: HarperCollins.

Darwin, C. (1877) Biographical sketch of an infant, *Mind*, 2: 285–94.

Davies, M. (1995) *Helping Children to Learn through a Movement Perspective*. London: Hodder & Stoughton.

Dewey, J. [1933 (1998)] *How We Think*. New York: Houghton Mifflin.

Diaz, R.M., Neal, C.J. and Amaya-Williams, M. (1990) The social origins of self-regulation, in L.C. Moll (ed.) *Vygotsky and Education*. Cambridge: Cambridge University Press.

Donaldson, M. (1987) *Children's Minds*. London: Fontana Press.

Dunn, J. (1993) *Young Children's Close Relationships*. London: Sage.

Dweck, C. and Leggett, E. (1988) A social-cognitive approach to motivation and personality, *Psychological Review*, 95(2): 256–73.

Edwards, C., Gandini, L. and Forman, G. (1998) *The Hundred Languages of Children*. London: JAI Press.

Engel, S. (1995) *The Stories Children Tell*. New York: Freeman and Co.

Gardner, H. (1991) *The Unschooled Mind*. London: Fontana.

Garvey, C. (1977) *Play*. Cambridge, MA: Harvard University Press.

Gelman, R. and Gallistel, C. (1978) *The Child's Understanding of Number*. Cambridge, MA: Harvard University Press.

Goldberg, S. (2000) *Attachment and Development*. London: Arnold.

Goldschmied, E. (1987) *Infants at Work* (video). London: National Children's Bureau.

Gopnik, A., Meltzoff, A. and Kuhl, P. (1999) *How Babies Think*. London: Weidenfeld & Nicolson.

Harris, P. (1989) *Children and Emotion*. Oxford: Blackwell.

Hobson, P. (2002) *The Cradle of Thought*. London: Macmillan.

Holland, P. (1999) Talk on 'Zero tolerance to superhero play', Pen Green Centre, Corby, Northants, April.

Holmes, J. (1993) *John Bowlby and Attachment Theory*. London: Routledge.

Holt, J. (1991) *Learning All the Time*. Ticknall: Lighthouse Books.

Isaacs, N. (1966) *The Growth of Understanding in the Young Child: A Brief Introduction to Piaget's Work*. Norwich: Fletcher & Sons.

Isaacs, S. [1930 (1966)] *Intellectual Growth in Young Children*. London: Routledge & Kegan Paul.

Isaacs, S. (1933) *Social Development in Young Children*. London: Routledge & Sons.

Isaacs, S. (1952) The nature and function of phantasy, in J. Riviere (ed.) *Developments in Psychoanalysis*. London: Hogarth Press.

Katz, L. and Chard, S. (1989) Engaging Children's Minds: The Project Approach. Norwood, NJ: Ablex.

Kress, G. (1995) *Making Signs and Making Subjects: The English Curriculum and Social Futures*. London: Institute of Education.

Laevers, F. (1993) Deep Level Learning. *European Early Childhood Research*, Vol 1, No 1, pp. 53–68.

Laevers, F. (1994) The Innovative Project Experiential Education and the Definition of Quality in Education, *Studia Pedagogica, 16*, pp. 159–72.

Laevers, F. (1997) *A Process-Oriented Child Follow-up System for Young Children*, Centre for Experiential Education: Leuven University, Belgium.

Lally, M. (1991) *The Nursery Teacher in Action*. London: Paul Chapman.

Lee, V. and Das Gupta, P. (eds) (1995) *Children's Cognitive and Language Development*. Buckingham: Open University Press.

Light, P. and Barnes, P. (1995) Development in drawing, in V. Lee and P. Das Gupta (eds) *Children's Cognitive and Language Development*. Buckingham: Open University Press.

Maclellan, E. (1997) The importance of counting, in I. Thompson (ed.) *Teaching and Learning Early Number*. Buckingham: Open University Press.

Main, M. (1999) Epilogue: attachment theory, in J. Cassidy and P.R. Shaver (eds) *Handbook of Attachment*. New York: Guilford Press.

Marsh, J. and Hallet, E. (eds) (1999) *Desirable Literacies*. London: Paul Chapman.

Matthews, J. (1994) *Helping Children to Paint and Draw in Early Childhood*. London: Hodder & Stoughton.

McDonagh, J. and McDonagh, S. (1999) Learning to talk, talking to learn, in J. Marsh and E. Hallett (eds) *Desirable Literacies*. London: Paul Chapman.

Meade, A. with Cubey, P. (1995) *Thinking Children*, New Zealand Council for Educational Research: Wellington.

Rescorla, L. (1980) 'Overextension in Early Language Development', *Journal of Child Language*, **7**, pp. 321–35.

Schaffer, D. and Dunn, J. (eds) (1979) *The First Year of Life: Psychological and Medical Implications of Early Experience*. Chichester: Wiley.

Smart, C., Neale, B. and Wade, A. (2001) *The Changing Experiences of Childhood, Families and Divorce*. Cambridge: Polity Press.

Stern, D. (1985) *The Interpersonal World of the Infant*. New York: Basic Books.

Tizard, B. (1986) *The Care of Young Children: Implications of Recent Research*. London: Institute of Education.

Trevarthen, C. (2001) Talk on 'Tuning into children: motherese and teacherese', Pen Green Centre, Corby, Northants, March.

Trevarthen, C. (2002) Seminar with research team, Pen Green Centre, Corby, Northants, February.

Tulloch, S. (ed.) (1993) *Reader's Digest Oxford Complete Wordfinder*. Oxford: Reader's Digest.

Vygotsky, L.S. (1978) *Mind in Society*. London: Harvard University Press.

Vygotsky, L.S. (1986) *Thought and Language*. London: MIT Press.

Whalley, M. (ed.) (1997) *Working with Parents*. Sevenoaks: Hodder & Stoughton.

Whalley, M. (ed.) (2001) *Involving Parents in Their Children's Learning*. London: Paul Chapman.

Whalley, M. and Arnold, C. (1997) Parental involvement in education. Summary Paper. London: Teacher Training Agency.

Winnicott, D.W. (1975) *Through Pediatrics to Psychoanalysis*. London: Hogarth Press.

Winnicott, D. (1988) *Babies and Their Mothers*. London: Free Association Press.

Winnicott, D.W. (1990) *The Maturational Processes and the Facilitating Environment*. London: Karnac Books.

Index

Page numbers in *italics* refer to figures and tables.

STARTING FROM THE CHILD

Julie Fisher

Early years practitioners currently face a number of dilemmas when planning an education for young children. The imposition of an external curriculum seems to work in opposition to the principles of planning experiences which start from the child. Does this mean that the notion of a curriculum centred on the needs and interests of children is now more rhetoric than reality?

In a practical and realistic way Starting from the Child examines a range of theories about young children as learners and the implications of these theories for classroom practice. Julie Fisher acknowledges the competence of young children when they arrive at school, the importance of building on their early successes and the critical role of adults who understand the individual and idiosyncratic ways of young learners. The book addresses the key issues of planning and assessment, explores the place of talk and play in the classroom and examines the role of the teacher in keeping a balance between the demands of the curriculum and the learning needs of the child.

This is essential reading, not only for early years practitioners, but for all those who manage and make decisions about early learning.

Contents
Competent young learners – Conversations and observations – Planning for learning – The role of the teacher – Encouraging independence – Collaboration and cooperation – The place of play – The negotiated classroom – Planning, doing and reviewing – Evaluation and assessment – References – Index.

192pp   0 335 19556 3 (Paperback)   0 335 19557 1 (Hardback)

SUPPORTING CREATIVITY AND IMAGINATION IN THE EARLY YEARS

Bernadette Duffy

This book draws on the author's experience of promoting young children's creativity and imagination in a variety of settings over the last twenty years. The settings include home and centre based care and this book draws on the practical experience of adults living and working with children in these settings. The aim of the book is to use real life examples of young children's development and their growing competence to show the richness of their creativity and imagination. Children's development across a wide range of creative and imaginative experiences are outlined and ways of planning and assessing children's progress are discussed. Insights from research are used to inform practice.

This book is for all who take delight in the richness of young children's learning and want to find ways to extend their practice by supporting and promoting learning in a practical way.

Contents

Acknowledgements – Series preface – Introduction – Part one: What are creativity and imagination and why are they important? – The importance of creativity and imagination for society and young children – Defining creativity and imagination – Creative and imaginative areas of experience – Part two: How do creativity and imagination develop? – The development of creativity and imagination from birth to six years – The creative process – Part three: Theory into practice – The role of the adult – The organization of space, time and social contexts – Widening children's experiences – Planning, implementing, observing, recording and assessing – Conclusion – References – Index.

176pp   0 335 19871 6 (Paperback)   0 335 19872 4 (Hardback)